WALC™ 11: Language for H

Workbook of Activities for Languag...

by Kathryn J. Tomlin

Skills
- word finding
- organization
- categorization
- reasoning
- comprehension

Ages
- 16 and up

Grades
- high school and up

Evidence-Based Practice

According to the *Clinical Guidelines of The Royal College of Speech & Language Therapists* (www.rcslt.org/resources, 2005) and the National Stroke Association (2006), the following therapy principles are supported:

- Communication, both verbal and nonverbal, is a fundamental human need. Meeting this need by facilitating and enhancing communication in any form can be vital to a patient's well-being.
- Therapy should include tasks that focus on semantic processing, including semantic cueing of spoken output, semantic judgments, categorization, and word-to-picture matching.
- Therapy may target the comprehension and production of complex, as well as simple, sentence forms.
- Therapy should be conducted within natural communication environments.
- Rehabilitation is an important part of recovering from a stroke, and the goal is to regain as much independence as possible.

This book incorporates the above principles and is also based on expert professional practice.

LinguiSystems, Inc.
3100 4th Avenue
East Moline, IL 61244

FAX: 800-577-4555
Phone: 800-776-4332
E-mail: service@linguisystems.com
Web: linguisystems.com

Copyright © 2007 LinguiSystems, Inc.

All of our products are copyrighted to protect the fine work of our authors. You may only copy the client materials needed for your own use. Any other reproduction or distribution of the pages in this book is prohibited, including copying the entire book to use as another source or "master" copy.

The enclosed CD is for your personal use and convenience. It is unlawful to copy this CD or store its contents on a multi-user network.

Printed in the U.S.A.

ISBN 978-0-7606-0752-7

About the Author

Kathy and her therapy dog, Zanmi

Kathryn J. Tomlin, M.S., CCC-SLP, has been a speech-language pathologist in hospitals, rehabilitation centers, and long-term care facilities for over 25 years. Her materials, developed while working with clients, have evolved over the years. She has authored many materials with LinguiSystems over the last 20 years. Some of her works include:

The Source for Apraxia Therapy
WALC (Workbook of Activities for Language and Cognition) Series—
- *WALC 1: Aphasia Rehab (English and Spanish versions)*
- *WALC 2: Cognitive Rehab (English and Spanish versions)*
- *WALC 8: Word Finding*
- *WALC 9: Verbal and Visual Reasoning*
- *WALC 10: Memory*

Zanmi, Kathy's Samoyed, goes to work with her to encourage clients. Her clients enjoy feeding and spending time with Zanmi, and Zanmi enjoys their company. Everybody wins!

Dedication

This book is gratefully dedicated to my parents, who taught me to be a "jack of all trades." There are not enough words to thank you for all the lessons you taught me about keeping a home and about home maintenance. Your wisdom is now being shared with others through these activities.

Edited by Lauri Whiskeyman
Illustrations by Margaret Warner
Page layout by Jeanne Ketelaar
Cover design by Jason Platt

Table of Contents

	Home Activities	Home Maintenance Activities
Introduction		5
Word Finding	**8**	**97**
Naming Pictures	9	98
Matching Words to Pictures	12	101
Making Associations	15	104
Matching Words to Definitions	18	107
Naming Objects from Descriptions	21	110
Naming Wholes from Parts	24	113
Comparing Items	26	115
Listing Items for Tasks	28	117
Organization	**30**	**119**
Unscrambling Words	31	120
Unscrambling Sentences	34	123
Completing a Paragraph	37	126
Sequencing	41	130
Completing a Schedule	44	133
Categorization	**46**	**135**
Categorizing—Listing Items	47	136
Categorizing—Selecting 5 Items	50	139
Categorizing—Selecting Correct Items	52	141
Naming the Category	54	144
Reasoning	**57**	**147**
Making Word Deductions	58	148
Determining Category Exclusions	61	151
Completing Picture Analogies	63	153
Completing Sentence Analogies	65	155
Modifying Sentence Incongruities	67	157
Determining if Statements Are True or False	70	160
Comparing Sentence Content	75	165
Evaluating Information	78	168
Using Deductive Reasoning	83	173

Table of Contents, continued

	Home Activities	Home Maintenance Activities
Picture/Paragraph Comprehension	88	178
Answering Questions About a Picture	89	179
Comprehending Information in a Paragraph	94	184

Resources 187

Answer Key 190

Introduction

After a person suffers a neurological impairment to the brain, various language and cognitive skills are affected. Rehabilitation therapy can help retrain those skills. A client may rationalize that he has difficulty with tasks because he doesn't know the information to begin with or that the content of the task is not something he is interested in. To address this, the activities in *WALC 11: Language for Home Activities* were developed to provide stimulus items for remediation of language and cognitive-linguistic impairments that are relevant to a person's daily activities around the home. The tasks endeavor to make the content familiar to the client while retraining the foundation skills for language and cognitive processing, formulation, and expression.

The first section of this book addresses general knowledge associated with the home. The second section addresses general knowledge associated with home maintenance. A general assumption may be that women will identify more with the home activities in the first section and men will identify more with the home maintenance activities in the latter half of the book. However, this is not always the case. Part of the enjoyment of using these tasks will be the adventure you and your clients have learning about the topics they find interesting and relevant.

The following main skill areas provide the basis for *WALC 11*.

- **Word Finding**
  Providing the short-answer responses to the tasks will improve your client's word-retrieval skills. The tasks will stimulate the recall of information and words stored in your client's memory. They will also assist in the speed and accuracy of word retrieval.

- **Organization**
  The tasks in this book involve organization of thought (e.g., unscrambling words and sentences). Being able to think in a logical, organized manner will improve your client's ability to recall information, answer questions, make schedules, and reason effectively.

- **Categorization**
  Information is stored in the brain in a highly organized, logical manner. One of the storage and retrieval systems is categorization. Many of the tasks in this book will improve your client's ability to categorize. This will aid in his ability to comprehend, process information, and use data to formulate answers.

Introduction, continued

- **Reasoning**
  Many of the tasks in this book involve taking salient information and using it to deduce an answer. Some of the tasks involve overt reasoning (e.g., word deduction, analogies) and other tasks involve covert reasoning (e.g., sequencing sentences of an activity, determining part/whole relationships).

- **Picture/Paragraph Comprehension**
  Due to difficulties with visual reasoning, visual interpretation, and visual figure-ground perception, clients frequently do not interpret visual stimuli correctly. Tasks in this section use scenes to aid in a client's ability to relearn visual skills.

  Due to difficulties with memory and the ability to sustain information over time, a client frequently has difficulty interpreting information presented in paragraphs. Tasks that involve interpreting and responding to paragraph information improve a client's ability to retain and recall longer material.

There are many processes layered into each task in this book. Some of the processes are:

➤ **visual perception**: Tasks involving pictures aid a client's ability to perceive and interpret visually presented information. Information in some tasks is bolded to help your client key into content material.

➤ **thought organization**: Tasks involve interpreting stimuli and then devising a response. This will aid in reestablishing effective thought organization.

➤ **verbal rehearsal**: Initially, it will be helpful to have your client verbalize the task items and the processing he is using to determine the answers. As accuracy improves, encourage him to solve the problems silently, as silent thinking is much faster than thinking aloud.

➤ **attention/concentration**: It is important that your client be able to maintain attention to presented information over time. The tasks in this book address this by slowly increasing the amount of information presented, beginning with one word at a time, then sentences, paragraphs, and finally, narratives.

➤ **memory**: In order to determine a correct response, a client must remember all of the salient content presented in a task. A client must not only remember what was in the stimulus item but he must also remember his processing strategies and responses.

Introduction, continued

➤ **convergent and divergent thinking**: The format of the tasks in this book addresses convergent and divergent thinking. Questions that require short, specific answers involve convergent thinking. Questions that have more than one right answer or require recall of personal experience involve divergent thinking.

Suggestions for Use

1. Have the client read the tasks aloud initially to insure his processing is efficient and effective. Once the process is established, have him complete the tasks silently.

2. On tasks that require the client to choose an answer, it may be helpful to show one line at a time until he is comfortable with the format of the task.

3. Ask the client to read information or answers aloud or to repeat them after you to help him code the information.

4. A client may need your guidance to find the most effective method to complete a task.

5. Flexibility in thinking is challenged with tasks having more than one right answer. Accept any logical answers but guard against over generalization or the tendency to focus on the exceptions instead of the most obvious answers.

6. It may be beneficial to let the client observe you as you think through a task aloud so he can model your reasoning and thinking strategies.

7. Identify the strategies that are the most difficult for your client and emphasize them in therapy.

8. Answers are provided in the Answer Key. There are times when items have multiple answers even if only one is listed. Accept any reasonable answer as correct. Emphasize enjoyment rather than accuracy.

May you find these tasks as enjoyable to do with your clients as I did writing and revising them with my clients over the last 20+ years.

Kathy

Home Activities

The activities in the first half of this book address general knowledge associated with the home. The familiar and relevant content in the tasks will increase your client's interest as it taps into information stored in his remote memory. This will make your client feel like the tasks apply directly to him. These tasks are designed to utilize your client's foundational skills to improve language and cognitive processing, sentence formulation, and verbal expression.

Word Finding

Everyone has some degree of word-finding difficulty, but for someone who has a brain dysfunction, the frequency of anomic difficulties is intensified. A client will frequently attempt to rationalize that he cannot remember a word because it is not familiar to him. However, the familiarity of content in these tasks will increase your client's awareness that he indeed has difficulty with word finding and will encourage him to remediate the problem.

The tasks in this section address several layers of naming skills, including the following.

- confrontational naming
- making associations
- matching words to definitions
- naming objects from descriptions
- naming whole objects when given a part
- comparing items to determine which fit a superlative condition
- listing items from tasks

The tasks target word finding related to furniture, kitchen items, food, household items, and household tasks.

Naming Pictures

Name the pictures.

Naming Pictures

Name the pictures.

Naming Pictures

Name the pictures.

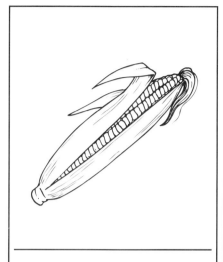 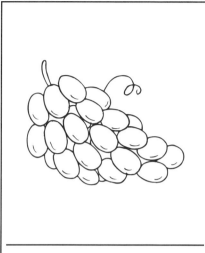 

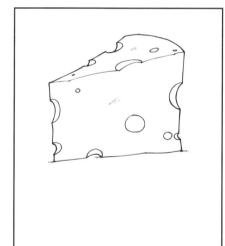  

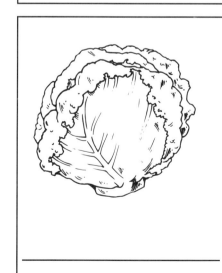  

Matching Words to Pictures

Find a word to match each picture. Draw a line from the word to the picture.

sofa

desk

lamp

picture

piano

Matching Words to Pictures

Find a word to match each picture. Draw a line from the word to the picture.

rolling pin

baking pan

pitcher

cutting board

pot

Matching Words to Pictures

Find a word to match each picture. Draw a line from the word to the picture.

Swiss cheese

bread

corn

grapes

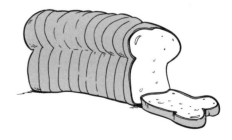

cake

Making Associations

Find a word on the left that goes with a word in the box. The first one is done for you.

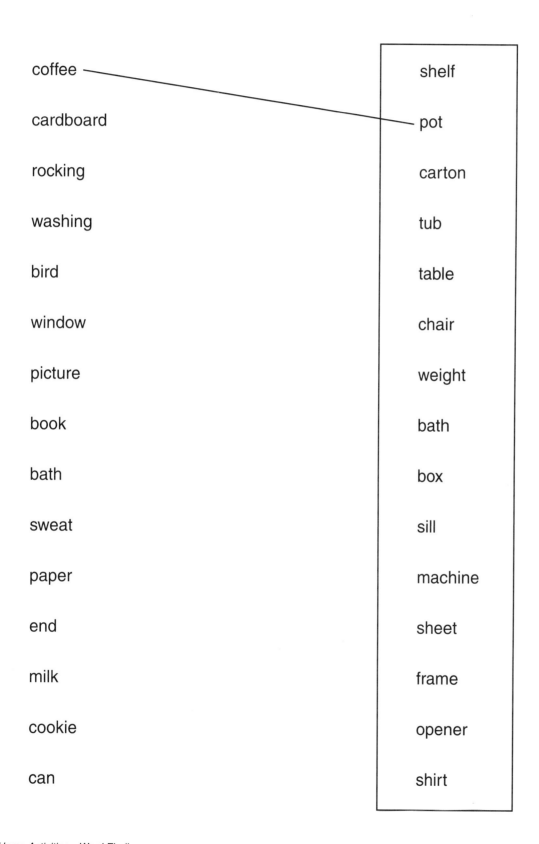

coffee ——————————— pot

cardboard

rocking

washing

bird

window

picture

book

bath

sweat

paper

end

milk

cookie

can

shelf

pot

carton

tub

table

chair

weight

bath

box

sill

machine

sheet

frame

opener

shirt

Making Associations

Find a word on the left that goes with a word in the box. The first one is done for you.

cheese —————————————→	jar
butcher	foil
soup	case
aluminum	shredder
pillow	spoon
shower	knife
frying	shaker
picnic	curtain
cookie	table
suit	bowl
salt	pan
coffee	bulb
hand	mug
mixing	case
light	mixer

Making Associations

Find a word on the left that goes with a word in the box. The first one is done for you.

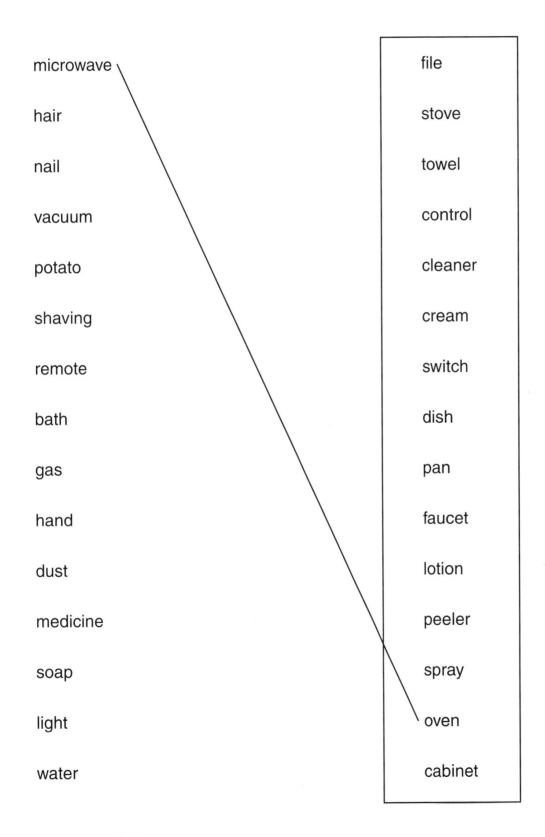

Left	Box
microwave	file
hair	stove
nail	towel
vacuum	control
potato	cleaner
shaving	cream
remote	switch
bath	dish
gas	pan
hand	faucet
dust	lotion
medicine	peeler
soap	spray
light	oven
water	cabinet

(microwave → oven)

Matching Words to Definitions

Match each word to its definition. Write the letter on the blank.

1. _____ sugar

2. _____ frame

3. _____ couch

4. _____ curtain

5. _____ tea

6. _____ sponge

7. _____ aluminum foil

8. _____ plunger

9. _____ flowers

10. _____ bandage

a. a covering for a window

b. used for wiping up a spill

c. put on a cut

d. used to unclog drains

e. a piece of furniture more than one person can sit on

f. a sweetener

g. used to cover or wrap food

h. goes around a picture

i. decorative plants for a garden

j. a beverage

Matching Words to Definitions

Match each word to its definition. Write the letter on the blank.

1. _____ mirror
2. _____ dresser
3. _____ iron
4. _____ oven
5. _____ ladle
6. _____ bookcase
7. _____ furniture polish
8. _____ steel wool pad
9. _____ bifocals
10. _____ yard

a. used to clean pans

b. used when dusting furniture

c. a type of eyeglasses

d. a kind of spoon used for serving soup

e. a piece of furniture used to store clothing

f. the property surrounding a house

g. an appliance used to take wrinkles out of fabric

h. an appliance that bakes food

i. shows your reflection

j. a piece of furniture containing several shelves

Matching Words to Definitions

Match each word to its definition. Write the letter on the blank.

1. _____ filing cabinet

2. _____ armchair

3. _____ can opener

4. _____ skillet

5. _____ coffeepot

6. _____ stove

7. _____ medicine cabinet

8. _____ shower

9. _____ closet

10. _____ cane

a. a place to hang coats

b. a pan used on the stove to fry food

c. a comfortable place to sit

d. a place to wash your body

e. used for brewing and serving a beverage

f. an appliance that heats the bottoms of pans to cook food

g. helps you keep your balance when walking

h. a place for storing pills, razor, and toothpaste

i. a container with sliding drawers

j. a device for opening cans

Naming Objects from Descriptions

What object is described?

1. This tree stays green all year. _____

2. This is used for cutting meat. _____

3. This is used to call your friends. _____

4. This is jewelry worn around the neck. _____

5. This is what people earn and spend. _____

6. This is a vehicle with a steering wheel. _____

7. This is used to hang a dress or pants. _____

8. This is used to gather groceries at the store. _____

9. This is used to sew on a button. _____

10. This is a common medicine for colds. _____

11. This is used to dry off after a shower. _____

12. This is used to get the tangles out of hair. _____

13. This is used to water a plant. _____

14. This is a piece of furniture with drawers. _____

15. This is a room to sleep in. _____

Naming Objects from Descriptions

What object is described?

1. This is what we walk on that is beside a street. _____

2. This is a book that contains recipes. _____

3. This kitchen utensil is used to flip pancakes. _____

4. This condiment is used on hot dogs or hamburgers. _____

5. This kind of store sells clothing, dishes, and many other things. _____

6. This is something hung on the wall for decoration. _____

7. This musical instrument has black and white keys. _____

8. This is a small bag used to carry money, keys, and other personal belongings. _____

9. This is a small brush used to clean teeth. _____

10. This is an appliance used to bake foods. _____

11. This soft object is used to support the head when sleeping. _____

12. This electrical appliance is used to mix ingredients together. _____

13. This appliance cleans clothing. _____

14. This meal is eaten in the morning. _____

15. This is something we write with. _____

Naming Objects from Descriptions

What object is described?

1. This shows news, movies, and programs. _____

2. This is used to water the lawn. _____

3. This shows your reflection when you are combing your hair. _____

4. This is an appliance that cools the air. _____

5. This is a warm article of clothing. _____

6. This is a container to hold water when you wash the floor. _____

7. This is a spice used to season food. _____

8. This is something to write on. _____

9. This piece of furniture seats one or more people. _____

10. This metal pan is used for baking cookies. _____

11. This garden tool is used to dig a hole. _____

12. This is a place to store clean sheets and towels. _____

13. This is a place to plant flowers and vegetables. _____

14. These are containers used to store flour, sugar, salt, etc. _____

15. This is used to fasten papers together. _____

Naming Wholes from Parts

Name an object associated with each part.

1. knob _____
2. page _____
3. leaf _____
4. shelf _____
5. pocket _____
6. burner _____
7. core _____
8. collar _____
9. stem _____
10. lenses _____
11. faucet _____
12. wheel _____
13. mattress _____
14. hands _____
15. hook _____

16. handle _____
17. cord _____
18. blade _____
19. drawer _____
20. wick _____
21. legs _____
22. eraser _____
23. ink _____
24. frame _____
25. brim _____
26. bristles _____
27. button _____
28. buckle _____
29. base _____
30. cushion _____

Naming Wholes from Parts

Name an object associated with each part.

1. lid _____
2. batteries _____
3. arms _____
4. zipper _____
5. spout _____
6. door _____
7. shade _____
8. screen _____
9. laces _____
10. seat _____
11. pocket _____
12. strap _____
13. switch _____
14. eye _____
15. bud _____

16. nails _____
17. curtains _____
18. trunk _____
19. tray _____
20. lock _____
21. nozzle _____
22. stamp _____
23. bone _____
24. fringe _____
25. sheets _____
26. holes _____
27. tail _____
28. branch _____
29. antenna _____
30. pit _____

Comparing Items

Circle the answer.

Which item is the _____

1.	**longest?**	pencil	yardstick	key
2.	**lightest?**	feather	bar of soap	book
3.	**oldest?**	infant	toddler	teenager
4.	**darkest?**	ginger ale	cola	water
5.	**strongest?**	rope	thread	rubber band
6.	**sweetest?**	cookie	lettuce	dinner roll
7.	**tallest?**	house	bush	person
8.	**hottest?**	blender	iron	vacuum
9.	**widest?**	road	table	ocean
10.	**loudest?**	screaming	talking	whispering
11.	**whitest?**	dirt	grass	snow
12.	**hardest?**	sugar	frying pan	dough
13.	**meanest?**	puppy	therapy dog	attack dog
14.	**softest?**	kitten	rock	sink
15.	**earliest?**	night	morning	evening

Comparing Items

Circle the answer.

Which item is the _____

1.	**shortest?**	toothpick	hairbrush	hanger
2.	**heaviest?**	stool	chair	sofa
3.	**youngest?**	boy	infant	grandfather
4.	**brightest?**	lamp	candle	mirror
5.	**crispiest?**	butter	lunch meat	potato chip
6.	**sourest?**	ice cream	dill pickle	tea
7.	**shortest?**	hour	second	day
8.	**coldest?**	ice	water	milk
9.	**thinnest?**	cracker	muffin	slice of bread
10.	**quietest?**	shouting	talking	whispering
11.	**blackest?**	cheese	licorice	chocolate
12.	**softest?**	dough	ice	rock candy
13.	**largest?**	bike	wagon	jet plane
14.	**greenest?**	lemon	lime	grapefruit
15.	**sharpest?**	steak knife	butter knife	spoon

Listing Items for Tasks

List four things you need for each activity.

Doing the Laundry

1. _____ 3. _____

2. _____ 4. _____

Paying the Bills

1. _____ 3. _____

2. _____ 4. _____

Caring for a Pet

1. _____ 3. _____

2. _____ 4. _____

Repotting a Plant

1. _____ 3. _____

2. _____ 4. _____

Listing Items for Tasks

List four things you need for each activity.

Making a Meal

1. _____ 3. _____

2. _____ 4. _____

Fixing Your Hair

1. _____ 3. _____

2. _____ 4. _____

Filling a Photo Album

1. _____ 3. _____

2. _____ 4. _____

Cleaning the Kitchen

1. _____ 3. _____

2. _____ 4. _____

Organization

The tasks in this section involve organization of thoughts. Being able to think in a logical, organized manner will improve your client's ability to take information and comprehend it in a hierarchical manner. This will help to negate the tendency to think divergently or to utilize mental manipulation in a manner that becomes tangential and off course. The tasks are organized as follows to stimulate this progression in thinking to achieve a desired goal.

- In tasks where your client unscrambles words, he first needs to recall word possibilities within the category and make an organized decision for which word is the correct item. Then he needs to order the letters correctly to form the word.

- When unscrambling words to make a sentence related to common household activities, completing paragraphs related to familiar events or activities, or sequencing the steps of an activity of daily living, your client must use the content in an organized, progressive manner.

- When completing the scheduling activities, your client must use the information presented in the paragraph and organize it based on content and on time sequence.

The content of the tasks in this section focuses on food, clothing, household items, and household activities.

Unscrambling Words

Unscramble each word. The first letter is capitalized and underlined.

Spices

1. l i <u>D</u> l
2. l v o <u>C</u> e s
3. e <u>G</u> g n i r
4. h m y <u>T</u> e
5. <u>B</u> l s i a
6. c i a l r <u>G</u>
7. t a <u>S</u> l
8. e g m <u>N</u> t u
9. e <u>P</u> r p e p
10. <u>S</u> e a g

Clothing

1. r <u>S</u> i h t
2. a t <u>P</u> n s
3. f <u>S</u> r a c
4. <u>S</u> o c s k
5. e h <u>S</u> o s
6. p <u>S</u> i l
7. <u>G</u> v o l s e
8. o t <u>C</u> a
9. <u>B</u> l e t
10. r <u>S</u> i k t

Unscrambling Words

Unscramble each word. The first letter is capitalized and underlined.

Things in a Kitchen

1. a s <u>P</u> n
2. o k <u>F</u> r
3. w o <u>B</u> l
4. u s p <u>C</u>
5. <u>J</u> r a s
6. i <u>S</u> n k
7. o l w e <u>T</u>
8. a <u>T</u> e l b
9. o <u>S</u> n o p
10. <u>S</u> e v t o

Things in a Bathroom

1. o l <u>T</u> w e
2. a o p <u>S</u>
3. u <u>T</u> b
4. a u r t <u>C</u> i n
5. r o r i <u>M</u> r
6. l c e <u>S</u> a
7. r m <u>H</u> p a e
8. <u>T</u> e u s i s s
9. i <u>S</u> n k
10. a z <u>R</u> o r

Unscrambling Words

Unscramble each word. The first letter is capitalized and underlined.

Things in a Living Room

1. o f <u>S</u> a
2. a <u>C</u> r p t e
3. l o <u>C</u> c k
4. p a m <u>L</u>
5. <u>P</u> s t a l n
6. n i u t <u>C</u> r a
7. o <u>B</u> s k o
8. a h r i <u>C</u>
9. <u>C</u> t s o l e
10. n <u>E</u> d a e <u>T</u> l b

Cooking Words

1. a k <u>B</u> e
2. l <u>B</u> i o
3. l i r o <u>B</u>
4. r w <u>B</u> o n
5. <u>R</u> s a o t
6. m e <u>S</u> m r i
7. r <u>W</u> a m
8. m t a <u>S</u> e
9. t <u>H</u> a e
10. o t <u>T</u> a s

Home Activities—Organization
WALC 11: Language for Home Activities   33   Copyright © 2007 LinguiSystems, Inc.

Unscrambling Sentences

Unscramble each sentence. The first word in the sentence is capitalized.

1. roses She the in put vase.
   _____

2. 350° the to oven Preheat.
   _____

3. the his on He button shirt sewed.
   _____

4. What dinner we for having are?
   _____

5. timer off the The went on oven.
   _____

6. for went We Chicago our to vacation.
   _____

7. the the to school kids for went she store After left.
   _____

8. Friday vacuums mornings on He downstairs.
   _____

9. bag vacuum a The new needed.
   _____

10. his to bedroom told his son He clean.
    _____

Unscrambling Sentences

Unscramble each sentence. The first word in the sentence is capitalized.

1. with think finished do chores your you be will When you?
   _____

2. door way Please on the your lock out.
   _____

3. vegetables their They in garden planted.
   _____

4. hours stuffed for The roasted turkey five.
   _____

5. vacuums always she Leona before dusts.
   _____

6. room the There closet no in was more.
   _____

7. enough everyone wasn't for milk There.
   _____

8. 3:00 Our gets after mail delivered.
   _____

9. they because plants drooping water The needed started.
   _____

10. under cleaning the sink The were supplies.
    _____

Unscrambling Sentences

Unscramble each sentence. The first word in the sentence is capitalized.

1. lit went When out candles some they the electricity.

2. dessert for apple made pie Jeff an.

3. food money Coupons buying you when save.

4. counter on a was box the tissues of There.

5. soup the was in salt There much too.

6. relatives their for They prepared dinner.

7. having dessert What we are for?

8. color should paint we bedroom the What?

9. windows you wash Would the please?

10. table the kitchen Put the on groceries.

Completing a Paragraph

Use the words in the box to fill in the blanks.

lightning	glad	louder	oil
storm	living	drawer	house
two	suddenly	flashlight	

The Storm

The _____ was becoming worse. It had been raining for _____ hours. The thunder was becoming _____ and the _____ more frequent. _____ the electricity went out in the _____. Sam and Anita lit two _____ lamps they had in the _____ room. They got the _____ out of a kitchen _____. They were _____ when the electricity came back on about 20 minutes later.

Completing a Paragraph

Use the words in the box to fill in the blanks.

bidders	knew	old	own
go	gift	home	sale
mornings	happy	newspaper	

Antique Shopping

Karl loved to _____ to antique auctions. Each week he checked the _____ for sales. He usually went on Saturday _____, but sometimes he went to an evening _____ if it was close to his _____. He loved to see all of the _____ "treasures" being sold to the highest _____. Sometimes he bought an item for his _____ home, but occasionally he was able to get something he _____ one of his family members would like as a _____. Even if he bought nothing, he went home feeling _____.

Completing a Paragraph

Use the words in the box to fill in the blanks.

several	bills	savings	food
kitchen	money	time	portion
income	oven	days	

Tax Refund

When the Mendozas got their _____ tax refund, they decided it was _____ to plan how to spend it. There were _____ things that needed to be repaired—the old _____ floor tile and the _____ that always overcooked the _____. The money could also help pay some of their medical _____. After discussing it for several _____, they finally decided to use a _____ of the money to pay medical bills. The _____ they had left would be put into their _____ account.

Completing a Paragraph

Use the words in the box to fill in the blanks.

suitcases	Andrew	ocean	sunny
vacation	ready	through	car
cat	newspaper	windows	

Vacation Time

Frank, Ann, and their children, Rebecca and _____, were getting ready to go on _____. They had rented a house on the _____. They spent two days packing their _____. Ann took their _____ to a friend to take care of him while they were gone. Frank went _____ the house to make sure all the _____ were locked. They called to suspend their _____ delivery for one week. Finally, they were _____ to leave. They put their suitcases in the _____ and headed for the _____ beach.

Sequencing

Put the following steps in the correct order by numbering them. Then, name the task.

Set A _____

_____ Get dressed.
_____ Clean up the kitchen.
_____ Shut off the alarm.
_____ Eat breakfast.
_____ Get up.

Set B _____

_____ Put on the blanket.
_____ Take off the dirty sheets.
_____ Put on the bedspread.
_____ Put on a clean top sheet.
_____ Put on a clean bottom sheet.

Set C _____

_____ Pour the coffee into the mug.
_____ Drink the coffee.
_____ Put the dirty mug in the sink.
_____ Add cream and sugar.
_____ Make the coffee.

Set D _____

_____ Dig up the soil.
_____ Pull out the weeds.
_____ Water the plants.
_____ Pick the vegetables.
_____ Plant the seedlings.

Sequencing

Put the following steps in the correct order by numbering them. Then, name the task.

Set A _____

_____ Eat the hamburgers.
_____ Make the hamburger patties.
_____ Put the hamburger patties on buns.
_____ Put the hamburger patties on the grill.
_____ Start the grill.
_____ Cook the hamburger patties.

Set B _____

_____ Get the window cleaner and paper towels.
_____ Decide to wash the windows.
_____ Dry the window.
_____ Put the window cleaner away.
_____ Wash the window.
_____ Clean any spots you missed.

Set C _____

_____ Sort the laundry into separate loads.
_____ Put the laundry away.
_____ Fold the laundry.
_____ Dry the laundry.
_____ Add the laundry soap.
_____ Put a load in the washer.

Set D _____

_____ Tie the top of the bag.
_____ Get a new garbage bag.
_____ Notice the garbage bag is full.
_____ Put a new bag in the garbage can.
_____ Put the full bag out for the garbage collectors.
_____ Pull the full bag out of the garbage can.

Sequencing

Put the following steps in the correct order by numbering them. Then, name the task.

Set A _____

_____ Wash your body.
_____ Get dressed.
_____ Dry yourself off.
_____ Get into the shower.
_____ Wash your hair.
_____ Turn on the water.
_____ Get out of the shower.

Set B _____

_____ Seal the envelope.
_____ Put the letter in the mailbox.
_____ Write a letter.
_____ Write your return address on the envelope.
_____ Address the envelope.
_____ Put the letter into an envelope.
_____ Put a stamp on the envelope.

Set C _____

_____ Put the car into gear.
_____ Get into the car.
_____ Look around to see if the road is clear.
_____ Walk out of the house.
_____ Drive away.
_____ Put the key into the ignition and start the car.
_____ Fasten your seatbelt.

Completing a Schedule

Use the clues to fill in Anna's schedule.

At 6:00 a.m., Anna **got up**. A half an hour later, she **ate breakfast**. She **raked leaves** at 7:00, and at 8:30, Anna went to **visit Rebecca**. One hour later, Anna and Rebecca went to **Dawn's house**. At noon, they had **lunch** and at 1:00 p.m. they **went swimming**. At 3:00 they **went home**. By 4:30 Anna and Rebecca were **watching a movie** on TV.

Time	Activity

Completing a Schedule

Use the clues to fill in Helen's schedule.

Before going to her dance class at 11:00, Helen had a two-hour business meeting with Ali and Jenna. After dance class, she had lunch with her brother, Frank, at noon. By one, she was shopping with Maria at the mall. After two hours, they were exhausted, so Helen drove home to watch a movie that started at 3:30. By 4:00 she was fast asleep in front of the TV.

Time	Activity
9:00	business meeting with Ali and Jenna
11:00	dance class
12:00	lunch with Frank
1:00	shopping with Maria at the mall
3:30	watch a movie
4:00	asleep in front of the TV

Categorization

Information is stored in the brain in a highly organized, logical manner. One of the systems we use for storage and retrieval is categorization. The tasks in this section will help your client reestablish categorizing strategies.

- Tasks that involve listing items needed to complete familiar activities will assist in recall of multiple words.

- Tasks that require your client to locate five words related to a given category provide the information as to how many words he must find. That information is not present in the next tasks where your client must locate multiple items that belong to a category without knowing exactly how many to find. This encourages language and cognitive processing and flexible thinking as your client determines which words belong to the given category.

- When naming the category, your client must use the categorizing skill in reverse order to determine how the task items are related.

The content of the tasks in this section focuses on cleaning items, appliances, rooms in a house, household items, and food.

Categorizing—Listing Items

List as many items as you can for each category.

Cleaning Items

1. _____ 5. _____
2. _____ 6. _____
3. _____ 7. _____
4. _____ 8. _____

Appliances

1. _____ 5. _____
2. _____ 6. _____
3. _____ 7. _____
4. _____ 8. _____

Rooms in a House

1. _____ 5. _____
2. _____ 6. _____
3. _____ 7. _____
4. _____ 8. _____

Categorizing—Listing Items

List as many items as you can for each category.

Cooking Items

1. _____   5. _____
2. _____   6. _____
3. _____   7. _____
4. _____   8. _____

Bathroom Items

1. _____   5. _____
2. _____   6. _____
3. _____   7. _____
4. _____   8. _____

Household Tasks

1. _____   5. _____
2. _____   6. _____
3. _____   7. _____
4. _____   8. _____

Categorizing—Listing Items

List as many items as you can for each category.

Spices

1. _____ 5. _____
2. _____ 6. _____
3. _____ 7. _____
4. _____ 8. _____

Furniture

1. _____ 5. _____
2. _____ 6. _____
3. _____ 7. _____
4. _____ 8. _____

Items in a Closet

1. _____ 5. _____
2. _____ 6. _____
3. _____ 7. _____
4. _____ 8. _____

Categorizing—Selecting 5 Items

Identify five words in each box associated with the word on the left.

TV	cord channels	telephone programs	news dress	movie water

Plant	chair water	plant food clock	dirt sunlight	rust pot

Mail	letters coaster	envelopes bills	hair delivered	stamps pizza

Suitcase	pack clothing	block handle	trip table	brick carry

Home	moon residence	roof yard	rooms pocket	basement wig

Lamp	pillow shade	snow light	bulb cord	switch bridge

Categorizing—Selecting 5 Items

Identify five words in each box associated with the word on the left.

Cereal	breakfast	cushion	milk	eat
	vinegar	bowl	crispy	vase

Chair	furniture	fan	sit	back
	leaves	legs	seat	avenue

Refrigerator	shelves	pants	cold	freezer
	oven	door	tile	crisper

Music	sleeve	melody	fry	floor
	harmony	notes	singer	radio

Shoes	heel	book	feet	peanuts
	sole	laces	garden	leather

Stove	pan	burner	freeze	rinse
	radio	cook	heat	dial

Categorizing—Selecting Correct Items

Identify the items that belong in each category.

Things in a Kitchen	gasoline plates glasses toilet	bowls milk sheets food	measuring cups coffee cup toothpaste dishes
Things Used to Wash Clothes	camera washer sponge water	basket dryer pots and pans shampoo	dirty clothes soda detergent fabric softener
Ingredients for a Salad	lettuce pumpkin tomatoes cereal	pork chop onion cucumber grass	radish bark flowers celery
Sewing Words	cloth stairs thread beef	pins needle scissors tape measure	mend limbs thimble patterns
Money Words	buns quarter brow nickel	dollar pinch sugar dime	half dollar penny collar block

Categorizing—Selecting Correct Items

Identify the items that belong in each category.

Pets	canary	eagle	horse
	hamster	dog	roach
	slug	cheetah	squirrel
	elephant	parrot	cat

Weather	snow	rain	drive
	hail	paper	sunny
	cover	clear	windy
	sleet	wiper	pike

Toys	ball	walk	teddy bear
	matches	doll	saw
	necktie	blocks	creamer
	truck	screen	puzzles

Plants	bucket	flower	cactus
	vine	dirt	bush
	grass	fern	shrub
	tree	garden	shovel

Things in a Bedroom	wagon	blanket	nightstand
	pillow	bed	wheel
	stove	alarm clock	eggs
	mirror	washer	dresser

Naming the Category

Name the category for each list of items.

1. salt, oregano, pepper, dill _____

2. teaspoon, ounce, cup, tablespoon _____

3. bathroom, kitchen, den, bedroom _____

4. pork, beef, ham, veal _____

5. shower, toilet, bathtub, medicine cabinet _____

6. plate, glass, silverware, napkin _____

7. laundry, vacuuming, cooking, dusting _____

8. fried, scrambled, omelet, soft-boiled _____

9. sofa, chair, dresser, cabinet _____

10. celery, radish, lettuce, corn _____

11. oak, pine, ash, willow _____

12. sheets, pillows, mattress pad, blanket _____

13. strawberries, bananas, apples, pears _____

14. cream, butter, milk, cheese _____

15. curtains, drapes, blinds, sheers _____

Naming the Category

Name the category for each list of items.

1. glass, cup, goblet, mug _____

2. lemon meringue, cherry, pumpkin, apple _____

3. pecans, almonds, pistachios, peanuts _____

4. rye, wheat, white, whole grain _____

5. brown, blonde, brunette, black _____

6. perch, bass, flounder, tuna _____

7. lemonade, water, iced tea, ginger ale _____

8. can, jar, bottle, carton _____

9. linoleum, carpet, hardwood, tile _____

10. twin, full, queen, king _____

11. toaster, can opener, microwave, coffee maker _____

12. shirt, pants, socks, skirt _____

13. candle, lamp, flashlight, sun _____

14. tulips, daisies, geraniums, pansies _____

15. oysters, clams, scallops, crabs _____

Naming the Category

Name the category for each list of items.

1. dog, cat, canary, parrot _____

2. slipper, shoes, socks, sneakers _____

3. rocker, recliner, chair, sofa _____

4. chicken, goose, turkey, duck _____

5. book, recipe, postcard, magazine _____

6. dime, quarter, dollar, nickel _____

7. Swiss, cheddar, mozzarella, American _____

8. fried, mashed, scalloped, baked _____

9. scissors, knife, razor, saw _____

10. chocolate layer, marble, angel food, yellow _____

11. cards, gifts, cake, party _____

12. comb, shampoo, brush, curlers _____

13. stem, roots, flower, leaves _____

14. hot dogs, baked beans, potato salad, chips _____

15. corduroy, wool, cotton, denim _____

Reasoning

The tasks in this section involve the skill of being able to use salient information to deduce an answer. To encourage thought flexibility as well as to discourage fixation, items within a task are not always uniform (e.g., some questions require a specific answer while others may have more than one right answer).

- When making word deductions, your client must reason how the words relate and utilize convergent reasoning to determine the answer.

- For category exclusion, your client must be able to compare and contrast multiple words to deduce which of the words does not belong with the others.

- Sentence and picture analogies involve deducing how the first pair of items are related and then carrying over that process so it is reflected in the second set of items.

- Identifying and then correcting incongruities in sentences involves verbal reasoning based on knowledge stored in your client's memory. Many of the sentences can be corrected in multiple ways, so it will require your client to make a determination as to which correction is best suited for the item according to his knowledge base.

- When determining if sentences are true or false, your client must be able to read the sentence, compare it to his knowledge, and then determine its correctness.

- For tasks involving comparing sentences to determine if they mean the same thing, your client needs to ascertain if word order affects the meaning or if the content in one sentence means the same as the other sentence. He must then make a determination based on grammar, word order, and content.

- The tasks for evaluating information incorporate a unique format in that they are more subjective. The items address things your client would or would not do depending upon his knowledge and background. This allows your client to have more freedom in his responses as they are based on his own personal preferences.

- The deductive reasoning tasks give practice using clues to determine which item fits the given content. They also incorporate an exclusion principle as it is easier to determine the answer by eliminating all unrelated items.

The content of the tasks in this section focuses on objects used around the home to complete familiar activities, home furnishings, household activities, and household chores.

Making Word Deductions

What item is described by the clue words?

1. cord, bag, suction, cleaning   _____

2. time, hands, wrist, numbers   _____

3. sweet, cane, white, spoonful   _____

4. cord, lightbulb, shade, switch   _____

5. cushions, living room, seats three, soft   _____

6. breakable, reflects, glass, wall   _____

7. plush, fibers, wall-to-wall, floor   _____

8. fast cooking, appliance, kitchen, timer   _____

9. sharp, blade, cut, handle   _____

10. shower, absorbent, rectangular, dry _____

11. closet, clothing, hang, rod   _____

12. frame, wall, artist, decoration   _____

13. kitchen, water, basin, faucet   _____

14. legs, wooden, furniture, flat top   _____

15. beverage, mug, caffeine, hot   _____

Making Word Deductions

What item is described by the clue words?

1. laces, sole, leather, feet _____

2. stir, soup, silverware, handle _____

3. bar, clean, slippery, washcloth _____

4. story, pages, cover, read _____

5. chicken, yolk, shell, omelet _____

6. collar, sleeves, clothing, buttons _____

7. teeth, paste, bristles, handle _____

8. screen, remote, shows, channels _____

9. plot, vegetables, flowers, weeds _____

10. sharp, sewing, threaded, metal _____

11. drive, transportation, gas, trunk _____

12. back, arms, cushion, sit _____

13. pills, pain reliever, two, headache _____

14. hands, wool, warm, winter _____

15. write, ink, ballpoint, paper _____

Making Word Deductions

What item is described by the clue words?

1. legs, cuffs, pockets, belt loops _____

2. temperature, glass, mercury, degrees _____

3. lenses, arms, see, bifocals _____

4. bed, feather, soft, head _____

5. tomatoes, condiment, bottle, burger _____

6. garden, long, flexible, water _____

7. cob, yellow, vegetable, kernel _____

8. call, ring, receiver, talk _____

9. water, cubes, frozen, drinks _____

10. petals, plant, stem, fragrance _____

11. sharpen, write, eraser, point _____

12. window, material, rod, covering _____

13. jewelry, finger, diamond, gold _____

14. mattress, sleep, covers, pillows _____

15. Italian, noodles, sauce, meatballs _____

Determining Category Exclusions

Mark the word that does not belong with the others.

1. shoes — hats — gloves — cars
2. pepper — noodles — cinnamon — salt
3. denim — sweater — wool — cotton
4. fork — gallon — quart — pint
5. bedroom — living room — carpeting — bathroom
6. split pea — pudding — tomato — chicken noodle
7. shower — tub — sink — workbench
8. hour — sun — minute — day
9. plate — bowl — newspaper — silverware
10. tea — coffee — plate — cocoa
11. swimming — dusting — vacuuming — cooking
12. napkins — tissues — paper plates — cans
13. pen — tack — pencil — marker
14. shoe — slipper — glove — sneaker
15. flounder — chicken — turkey — goose

Determining Category Exclusions

Mark the word that does not belong with the others.

1. dish towel — stove — refrigerator — mixer
2. breakfast — tuna — lunch — dinner
3. dresser — bed — sink — mirror
4. milk — bagel — biscuit — muffin
5. bench — chair — sofa — brush
6. bedspread — carpet — blanket — sheets
7. jacket — coat — sweater — socks
8. walls — dishes — windows — floors
9. skirt — pants — curtains — shirt
10. tree — tulip — daffodil — daisy
11. scissors — knives — razors — zippers
12. scrambled — hard-boiled — toast — fried
13. attic — alley — porch — basement
14. recliner — sofa — loveseat — drapes
15. needle — slicer — thread — thimble

Completing Picture Analogies

Circle the picture on the right that solves each analogy.

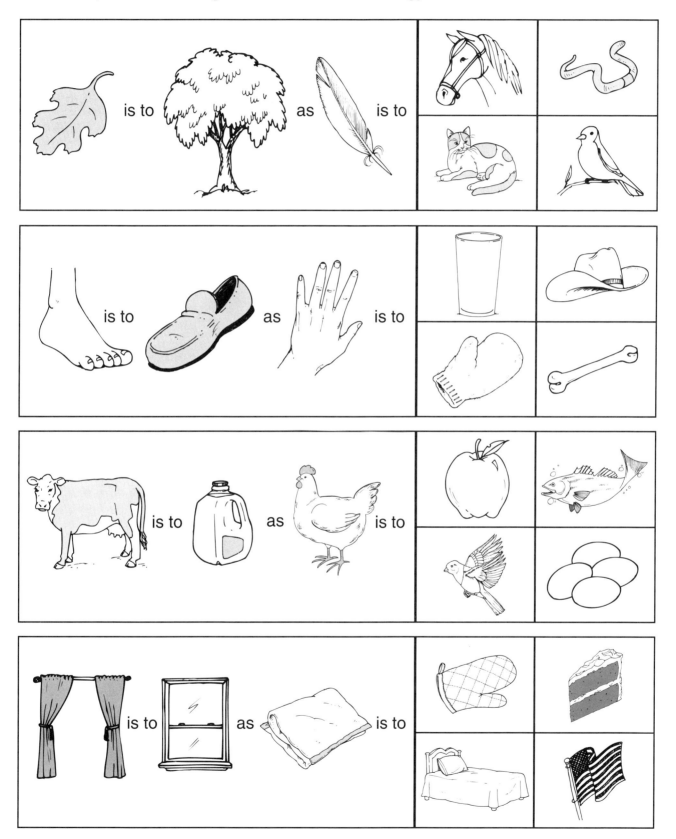

Completing Picture Analogies

Circle the picture on the right that solves each analogy.

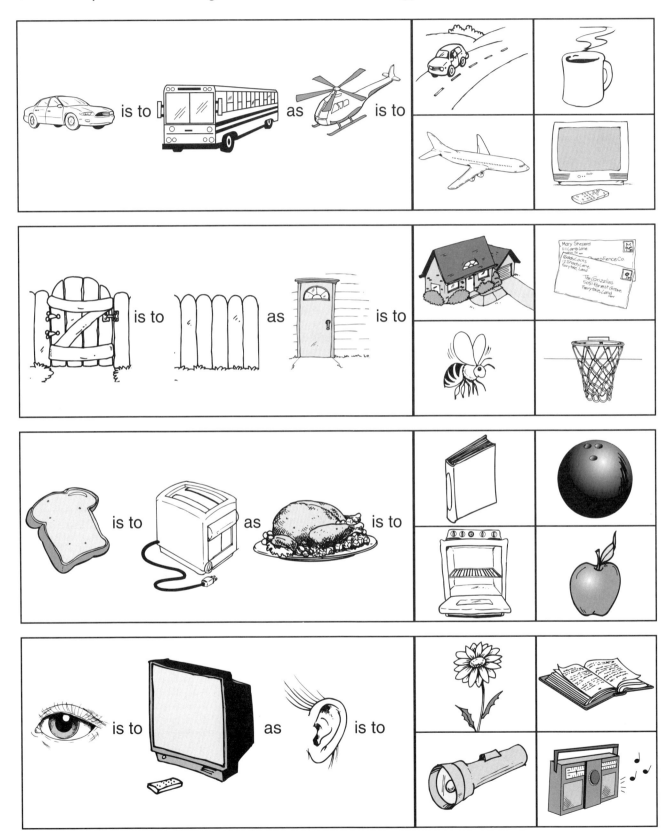

Completing Sentence Analogies

Complete the analogies.

1. A tablecloth is put on a table; a rug is put on the _____.

2. A handle is on a pot; a knob is on a _____.

3. White is the color of salt; black is the color of _____.

4. You fry a hamburger; you bake a _____.

5. Jokes are found in a joke book; recipes are found in a _____.

6. A book is for reading; a TV is for _____.

7. Legs are part of a table; cushions are part of a _____.

8. Beef is part of a stew; lettuce is part of a _____.

9. Hair is combed; teeth are _____.

10. Milk is a dairy product; beans are a _____.

11. A wick is part of a candle; a bulb is part of a _____.

12. A jar contains applesauce; a can contains _____.

13. Dishwashers clean dishes; washing machines clean _____.

14. Furniture is dusted; carpets are _____.

15. Coffee tastes bitter; sugar tastes _____.

Completing Sentence Analogies

Complete the analogies.

1. Cold water is used in iced tea; hot water is used in _____.

2. A drink is served in a glass; food is served on a _____.

3. A couch is in a living room; a bed is in a _____.

4. Candy tastes sweet; a lemon tastes _____.

5. A rug is put on the floor; a blanket is put on the _____.

6. A spoon is used for eating soup; a fork is used for eating _____.

7. A bulb is part of a lamp; a battery is part of a _____.

8. Pins are used in fabric; a staple is used on _____.

9. Prongs are part of a fork; a blade is part of a _____.

10. You fry on a burner; you bake in an _____.

11. Ice cream is cold; pizza is _____.

12. White is the color of cauliflower; green is the color of _____.

13. A bathtub is for bathing; a sink is for _____.

14. A razor is used for shaving; soap is used for _____.

15. Macaroni is used in macaroni salad; potatoes are used in _____.

Modifying Sentence Incongruities

Replace a word or phrase in each sentence that doesn't make sense.

1. She stored ice cream in the cupboard.

2. They had dinner at six o'clock in the morning.

3. He bought some lumber at the grocery store.

4. The children got home from school just before three in the morning.

5. When her car broke down, Judy called the emergency plumbing service.

6. They closed all the drawers when the rain started.

7. He put salt in his coffee.

8. When the bag was empty, she put a new one in the vacuum cleaner.

9. The zipper on the dresser was stuck.

10. His watch stopped working, so he replaced the band.

Modifying Sentence Incongruities

Replace a word or phrase in each sentence that doesn't make sense.

1. Milk is stored in a canister on the counter.

2. She planted a maple tree in the flower box.

3. He decided not to use the lamp because the bulb was frayed.

4. She used nail polish to dust the furniture.

5. The extra tissues are kept in the kitchen sink.

6. She put clean washcloths on the bed once a week.

7. The curtains covered the pictures.

8. The cake needed to be baked for ten minutes at 350°.

9. When the electricity went on, the flashlight came in handy.

10. They decided to have hamburgers for dessert.

Modifying Sentence Incongruities

Replace a word or phrase in each sentence that doesn't make sense.

1. The flower bulbs grew in the winter.
   _____

2. Jasmine said she would bake a chocolate or pickle cake.
   _____

3. He dug up the dirt in the living room with a shovel.
   _____

4. She used a rake to flip the pancakes.
   _____

5. The man put two cups of sugar on his cereal.
   _____

6. He washed the windows with a broom.
   _____

7. She used a strainer to cook the spaghetti.
   _____

8. Preheat the oven to 650° to roast the chicken.
   _____

9. They went to the library to buy aspirin.
   _____

10. The neighbors sprinkled sugar on the sidewalk to melt the ice.
    _____

Determining if Statements Are True or False

Write **T** on the line if the statement is true. Write **F** if the statement is false.

_____ 1. Chili powder is often used in cake mixes.

_____ 2. A tub, toilet, and sink are usually found in a bathroom.

_____ 3. It's important to check the oil in your car regularly.

_____ 4. It's not necessary to sort clothing before washing.

_____ 5. Bottles, garbage, cans, and eggshells can be recycled.

_____ 6. Potato peels can be ground in the garbage disposal.

_____ 7. Aluminum foil is shiny.

_____ 8. Spices and seasoning add flavor to food.

_____ 9. Furniture polish completely prevents furniture from getting dusty.

_____ 10. A bed pillow is filled with large pieces of plastic.

_____ 11. Cheese is made from eggs, water, and vinegar.

_____ 12. Plants need water and sunlight to grow.

_____ 13. A clock usually has five or six hands.

_____ 14. Paper towels can be used to clean up spills.

_____ 15. Lettuce and tomatoes are unhealthy foods to eat.

Determining if Statements Are True or False

Write **T** on the line if the statement is true. Write **F** if the statement is false.

_____ 1. Pickle relish can be eaten with hamburgers and hot dogs.

_____ 2. Air conditioners cool the air in hot weather.

_____ 3. You should shampoo your carpets daily.

_____ 4. Most trees lose their leaves in the fall.

_____ 5. Oil and grease are easy to wash out of clothing.

_____ 6. A garbage disposal is located below a kitchen sink.

_____ 7. Flour and sugar must be kept in the freezer.

_____ 8. You can freeze meats and vegetables.

_____ 9. Pineapples are used in spaghetti sauces.

_____ 10. Paprika, oregano, and ginger are spices.

_____ 11. Many people preheat the oven before baking.

_____ 12. Some people have telephone answering machines.

_____ 13. Pepper helps melt the ice on sidewalks in the winter.

_____ 14. An omelet is made with eggs.

_____ 15. Many ovens have timers to tell you when baked goods are done.

Determining if Statements Are True or False

Write **T** on the line if the statement is true. Write **F** if the statement is false.

_____ 1. Dark and white clothes should be washed together in hot water.

_____ 2. Some silver and brass items need to be polished.

_____ 3. Pans need to be washed after something is cooked in them.

_____ 4. Taking two aspirins will bring on a fever.

_____ 5. Spaghetti softens when it is boiled.

_____ 6. Hair and soap can clog drains.

_____ 7. It is recommended that you eat red meat every day.

_____ 8. Window screens help to keep the bugs out.

_____ 9. It is necessary to wear a heavy coat in the summer.

_____ 10. A chair seats one person and a sofa seats two or three.

_____ 11. Daily newspapers are delivered once a week.

_____ 12. Artificial flower arrangements need watering.

_____ 13. You should rinse your hair after shampooing it.

_____ 14. Split seams cannot be repaired.

_____ 15. Grass grows faster in the spring than in the winter.

Determining if Statements Are True or False

Write **T** on the line if the statement is true. Write **F** if the statement is false.

_____ 1. Curtains and drapes can be used for window coverings.

_____ 2. A carpeted floor is easier to scrub than linoleum.

_____ 3. Many people change their bed sheets once a week.

_____ 4. A sink can be found in the kitchen.

_____ 5. It takes less than an hour to bake a stuffed turkey.

_____ 6. A sponge holds more water than a bucket.

_____ 7. Some plants have flowers and others don't.

_____ 8. Magazine articles are usually longer than a novel.

_____ 9. Saltwater taffy is chewy.

_____ 10. Pickles are made from onions, carrots, and radishes.

_____ 11. English is read from left to right.

_____ 12. Pillowcases are used to cover pillows.

_____ 13. A hallway joins one room to another.

_____ 14. Most people wear sunglasses on dark, rainy days.

_____ 15. You receive an electrical bill in the mail every day.

Determining if Statements Are True or False

Write **T** on the line if the statement is true. Write **F** if the statement is false.

_____ 1. Tomatoes are green before they ripen.

_____ 2. The weather forecast can be helpful when planning your day's activities.

_____ 3. A dish towel is used to dry dishes and glasses.

_____ 4. There are ten quarts in a gallon of milk.

_____ 5. Some people use plant food to help plants stay healthy.

_____ 6. A doorbell tells you when you are getting a phone call.

_____ 7. Many men shave every morning.

_____ 8. Glasses sometimes get spots in the dishwasher.

_____ 9. Some stoves run on gas; some run on electricity.

_____ 10. Refrigerated food will never spoil.

_____ 11. Whole milk has no fat in it.

_____ 12. Sometimes stores have items on sale.

_____ 13. Prescription drugs can be bought over the counter.

_____ 14. You should never lock the door when you leave home.

_____ 15. Sugar, salt, and flour can be stored in canisters.

Comparing Sentence Content

Write **S** on the line if the sentences mean about the same. Write **D** if the sentences have different meanings.

_____ 1. Mail is delivered Monday through Saturday.
The mail is delivered every day except Sunday.

_____ 2. After they ate salad, they had soup and sandwiches.
They had soup and salad for dinner.

_____ 3. No one felt like cooking, so they went out to eat.
They went to a fast-food restaurant because they were in a hurry.

_____ 4. Everyone was uncomfortable because it was hot and humid.
The heat and humidity made it uncomfortable for everyone.

_____ 5. What time do you think they will arrive?
When do you expect them to arrive?

_____ 6. The lamp wouldn't stay lit.
The lightbulb in the lamp flickered on and off.

_____ 7. Al doubled the ingredients.
Al halved the ingredients.

_____ 8. He likes to read before going to sleep.
Before sleeping, he enjoys reading.

_____ 9. It was twenty minutes after eleven.
The time was eleven forty.

_____ 10. There was a half-dozen eggs in the carton.
There were six eggs in the carton.

Comparing Sentence Content

Write **S** on the line if the sentences mean about the same. Write **D** if the sentences have different meanings.

_____ 1. When the sun was directly overhead, they had lunch.
   They had their lunch at noon.

_____ 2. The cake sank in the middle when she opened the oven door.
   She opened the oven door to see if the cake was done.

_____ 3. You can make a new lining by using the old one for a pattern.
   By using the old lining as a pattern, you can make a new lining.

_____ 4. She was on page 192 of her favorite book.
   She was halfway through the book.

_____ 5. Last night he brought the dog in at 10:00.
   No one remembered to bring the dog in last night.

_____ 6. No one, except Dad, likes to mow the lawn.
   Dad enjoys mowing the lawn.

_____ 7. He slept until the alarm went off.
   When the alarm went off, he woke up.

_____ 8. The picture is hanging crooked.
   Someone needs to hang this picture.

_____ 9. Their favorite TV show comes on at 8:00 p.m.
   There are many shows they like to watch in the evening.

_____ 10. She puts milk and sugar in her coffee.
   She does not drink coffee without milk and sugar in it.

Comparing Sentence Content

Write **S** on the line if the sentences mean about the same. Write **D** if the sentences have different meanings.

_____ 1. The snowdrifts were over three feet high.
　　　　　It snowed so much that the drifts were above our waists.

_____ 2. She cleaned the bathroom last Tuesday.
　　　　　She cleaned the whole house last week.

_____ 3. Please clean up after you eat.
　　　　　Be sure to clean up when you're finished eating.

_____ 4. Flowers bloom in the spring and summer.
　　　　　Trees lose their leaves in the fall.

_____ 5. My mom, not my sister, is coming with me.
　　　　　Even though my mom is joining me, my sister is not coming.

_____ 6. The bus stops at the corner of Third and Main.
　　　　　The bus makes a stop at every other corner.

_____ 7. The flower shop had a sale on roses.
　　　　　The flower shop had a storewide sale.

_____ 8. Glass and plastic are recycled every Tuesday night.
　　　　　Every Tuesday night, glass and plastic are recycled.

_____ 9. Tony is allergic to citrus fruits.
　　　　　Tony is allergic to apples and pears.

_____ 10. When the whistle blew, it was time to go.
　　　　　 It was time to leave when we heard the whistle blow.

Evaluating Information

Write **Yes** on the blank if it is something you would do when **doing laundry**.
Write **No** if it is not something you would do.

_____ 1. Use fabric softener or dryer sheets.

_____ 2. Dry each load for about three hours.

_____ 3. Pack the clothes tightly in the washer.

_____ 4. Wash the dark clothes separately from the whites.

_____ 5. Add bleach to all of the loads.

_____ 6. Use bleach with only white clothes.

_____ 7. Add detergent to the wash cycle.

_____ 8. Use 4 or 5 cups of detergent to wash each load.

_____ 9. Clean the lint from the dryer filter.

_____ 10. Dry the clothes a day or two after washing them.

_____ 11. Fold the clothes after they are dried.

_____ 12. Carry the load of clothes to your bedroom.

_____ 13. Hang pants, shirts, socks and shoes in the closet.

_____ 14. Sort and match up pairs of socks.

_____ 15. Iron clothes that are wrinkled.

Evaluating Information

Write **Yes** on the blank if it is something you would do to **lose weight**.
Write **No** if it is not something you would do.

_____ 1. Discuss your plans with your doctor.

_____ 2. Keep track of the calories that you eat.

_____ 3. Weigh yourself twice a day.

_____ 4. Eat as many carbohydrates as you can.

_____ 5. Stop using all seasonings and spices.

_____ 6. Cut out sweets.

_____ 7. Try to change your eating habits.

_____ 8. Have one dessert instead of two.

_____ 9. Stop eating breakfast and lunch; only eat dinner.

_____ 10. Reduce your fat intake.

_____ 11. Drink several glasses of water before a meal.

_____ 12. Reduce the size of your food portions.

_____ 13. Eliminate between-meal snacks.

_____ 14. Join a group that helps with weight loss.

_____ 15. Reward yourself for reaching your goal.

Evaluating Information

Write **Yes** on the blank if it is something you would do when **making dinner**. Write **No** if it is not something you would do.

_____ 1. Make sure you know how many people will be eating dinner.

_____ 2. Plan what you want to have to eat.

_____ 3. Cook foods that are full of salt and high in calories.

_____ 4. Have food that people will like.

_____ 5. Plan to have several kinds of meat and maybe a vegetable.

_____ 6. Plan to have a balanced meal.

_____ 7. Set the table.

_____ 8. Give each person a napkin.

_____ 9. Listen to the weather forecast.

_____ 10. Choose some loud rock music for background sound.

_____ 11. Clean out the refrigerator.

_____ 12. Cook the food.

_____ 13. Let everyone know what time you will be eating.

_____ 14. Light the candles on the table.

_____ 15. Put leftovers in containers and put them in the fridge.

Evaluating Information

Write **Yes** on the blank if it is something you would do when the **electricity goes off**. Write **No** if it is not something you would do.

_____ 1. Get out a flashlight.

_____ 2. Light some candles.

_____ 3. Start a fire in every room.

_____ 4. Light oil lamps.

_____ 5. Check the circuit breaker.

_____ 6. Look outside to see if your neighbors' lights are out.

_____ 7. Call your friends in another state to see if their lights are out.

_____ 8. Call the electric company and report a problem.

_____ 9. Turn off the appliances that were on when the lights went out.

_____ 10. Light a fire in the fireplace.

_____ 11. Sit in the dark and do nothing.

_____ 12. Call an electrician to rewire your house.

_____ 13. Replace all of the lightbulbs in the lamps.

_____ 14. Get angry at the electric company.

_____ 15. Go to bed.

Evaluating Information

Write **Yes** on the blank if it is something you would do when you **drive**.
Write **No** if it is not something you would do.

_____ 1. Go 20 MPH below the speed limit to conserve gas.

_____ 2. Use your horn a lot to warn people to stay away.

_____ 3. Fasten your seatbelt.

_____ 4. Keep one foot on the brake and the other on the gas pedal.

_____ 5. Make sure you use your turn signals properly.

_____ 6. Make sure your registration is up to date.

_____ 7. Keep to the speed limit.

_____ 8. Only go 5 to 10 MPH over the speed limit.

_____ 9. Pass only on the right.

_____ 10. Speed up to get through yellow lights before they turn red.

_____ 11. Make sure your tires are in good condition.

_____ 12. Have adequate insurance coverage.

_____ 13. Know the rules of the road.

_____ 14. Keep an eye on the other drivers and drive defensively.

_____ 15. Assume that you always have the right-of-way.

Using Deductive Reasoning

Draw the objects on the shelf.

1. An old jug is in the center of the shelf.

2. A pair of candlesticks are side by side on the far right end.

3. Between the jug and the candlesticks are a small basket and a picture. The picture is to the left of the basket.

4. On the other end of the shelf is a ceramic pitcher.

5. A clock is between the jug and the pitcher.

Using Deductive Reasoning

Use the clues to determine which mug is on sale. Cross off mugs until you are left with one. The mug that is left is the one on sale.

1. The mug on sale doesn't have a floral design.

2. The mug on sale has a design on it.

3. The mug with hearts isn't for sale.

4. The mug on sale doesn't have diagonal lines.

5. The mug on sale doesn't make you think of music.

Which mug is on sale? _____

Using Deductive Reasoning

Use the clues to determine which is Myrtle's pet. Cross off the animals it can't be until you are left with one. The one that is left is Myrtle's pet.

1. Myrtle has always been afraid of rodents. She would never have a pet that looks like a mouse or a rat.

2. She has trouble walking, so she does not have a pet that needs to be walked.

3. She has always thought that birds are too messy, so she doesn't have a pet bird.

4. Her pet is a solid color.

Which pet is Myrtle's? _____

Using Deductive Reasoning

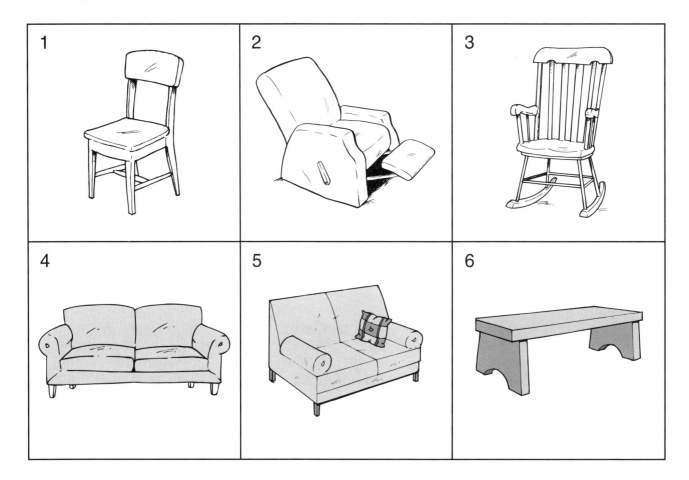

Trisha is trying to decide what to buy for her living room. Use the clues to determine what she bought. Cross off furniture until you are left with one. The one that is left is what Trisha bought.

1. She needed something to cover a spot on the wall, so it had to have a back.

2. Trisha thought that the straight back chair was too uncomfortable, so she didn't buy it.

3. The furniture that Trisha chose seated only one person.

4. She always loved rocking chairs because her mother had one, but she knew her husband wouldn't find a rocker comfortable when he was watching TV.

Which one did Trisha buy? _____

Using Deductive Reasoning

1 Trip to Disney World	2 Visit the relatives in another state	3 Stay home and do day trips
4 Camping trip to a state park in the mountains	5 Humanitarian trip to assist in the rebuilding in a hurricane devastated area	6 Trip to Europe

Joe and Mary Smith and their two teenage sons are discussing what they should do for their summer vacation. Use the clues to determine what they decided to do. Cross off the choices until you are left with one. The one left is what they chose.

1. Money was a little short, so they knew they couldn't fly overseas.

2. The last thing Joe wanted to do was spend a lot of time with relatives.

3. Mary strongly expressed that she didn't want to deal with the bugs on a camping trip.

4. All four felt like they wanted to get away from the house for their vacation.

5. As they had been to Disney World before, they decided not to go there again this trip.

6. The boys said they wanted to do something meaningful and lasting.

Where did they choose to go? _____

Picture/Paragraph Comprehension

People who experience some form of brain dysfunction often have difficulty with visual skills. They may have trouble interpreting what they see. They may have difficulty ascertaining specific items in a picture from the picture as a whole. They may have visual-spatial difficulties and be unable to determine where the items in a picture are in relation to the other items. Thus, this section presents several pictures with questions that target those difficulties to provide a structured approach for assisting in remediation of those skill areas.

Frequently, your client may be able to comprehend, manipulate, and deduce answers for stimuli that involves only a few words or a sentence, but his skills deteriorate as the length is increased to the paragraph level. This section includes paragraph comprehension tasks in order to help your client improve his ability to comprehend and retain lengthier written information.

The tasks in this section provide pictures related to painting and home repairs. The paragraphs relate to home repair situations your client may have or may encounter.

Answering Questions About a Picture

Look at the picture and answer the questions.

1. How many stories does the house have? _____

2. What is the number on the house? _____

3. What is between the sidewalk and the road? _____

4. What is around the property's border? _____

5. Can you see any gates? _____

6. Is smoke coming out of the chimney? _____

7. What shape is the window above the door? _____

8. How many windows can you see? _____

9. What is hanging from the tree? _____

10. What is in the backyard? _____

Answering Questions About a Picture

Look at the picture and answer the questions.

1. What time of day is it? _____

2. What furniture is in the room? _____

3. What is on the couch? _____

4. What is above the couch? _____

5. What room is near the living room? _____

6. What is near the window? _____

7. Is the TV on? _____

8. What kind of chair is in the room? _____

9. What is on the back of the chair? _____

10. What is lying on the chair? _____

Answering Questions About a Picture

Look at the picture and answer the questions.

1. How many chairs are there? _____

2. What is on the wall? _____

3. What time is it? _____

4. Is it before or after the meal? _____

5. How many places are set? _____

6. What food is being served? _____

7. Is there a tablecloth on the table? _____

8. Is there a sink in the picture? _____

9. What kitchen appliance can you see? _____

10. What is on the stove? _____

Answering Questions About a Picture

Look at the picture and answer the questions.

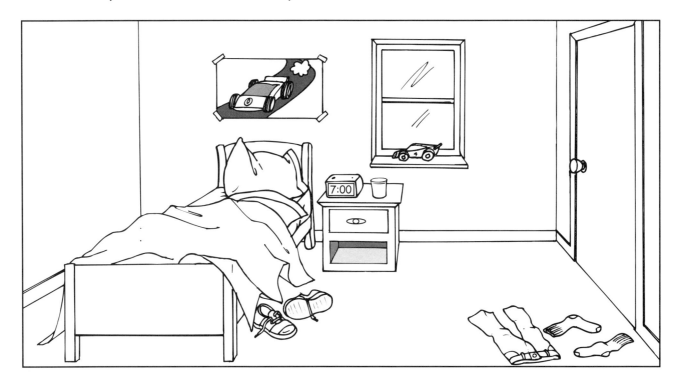

1. Is the bed made? _____

2. What is the bed near? _____

3. What is on the floor beside the bed? _____

4. What else is on the floor? _____

5. What is taped to the wall? _____

6. Are there curtains on the window? _____

7. What time is it? _____

8. What is beside the alarm clock? _____

9. Is the door open or shut? _____

10. What is on the windowsill? _____

Answering Questions About a Picture

Look at the picture and answer the questions.

1. What does the sidewalk lead to? _____
2. What toy is near the alley? _____
3. What is climbing up the tree? _____
4. What is someone planting? _____
5. What shape is the garden? _____
6. What tools are near the garden? _____
7. What kind of garden is it going to be? _____
8. Are the flowers planted or unplanted? _____
9. How many flowers are going to be planted? _____
10. What is coming down? _____

Comprehending Information in a Paragraph

Read the paragraph and answer the questions.

> It was Saturday morning and Vernon decided to do some chores. He dusted and started to vacuum the living room. The corner of the throw rug got caught in the vacuum roller. There was a loud noise accompanied by the smell of burning rubber. Vernon quickly turned the vacuum off, dislodged the rug, and inspected the vacuum. The vacuum belt was torn, so he replaced it with the spare belt he kept in the kitchen drawer. Vernon decided to finish vacuuming later in the week.

1. What day was it?

2. What chore did Vernon do first?

3. What chore did he do second?

4. What got caught in the vacuum roller?

5. What odor did he smell?

6. What had happened?

7. Where did Vernon keep the spare belt?

8. Who replaced the belt?

9. When did Vernon decide to finish vacuuming?

10. Has anything like this ever happened to you? What did you do?

Comprehending Information in a Paragraph

Read the paragraph and answer the questions.

> It was a typical crazy morning. Everyone was getting up to start their day at school or work, and there were the usual negotiations to see who got the bathroom next. After everyone was dressed, they came to the kitchen. Mom and Dad drank coffee and ate bagels and fruit as they packed school lunches. The children ate bowls of cereal in a hurry. A few minutes before the bus arrived, the children grabbed their books and lunches and rushed out the door. Then, Mom and Dad cleaned up the kitchen and drove to work.

1. Which days of the week could this be happening?

2. What negotiations took place?

3. What did everyone do before they went to the kitchen?

4. What did Mom and Dad have for breakfast?

5. How do you know there is more than one child in the family?

6. What did the children eat for breakfast?

7. What two things did the children take on the bus?

8. Who cleaned up the kitchen?

9. What was the last thing Mom and Dad did?

10. What are weekday mornings like in your home?

Comprehending Information in a Paragraph

Read the paragraph and answer the questions.

> Andy decided to make an apple pie for dessert because he was having company for dinner. First, he preheated the oven to 450°. Then, he pared and sliced six cups of apples and put them in a bowl. He sprinkled brown sugar, cornstarch, cinnamon, and nutmeg over the apples until they were well coated. Then, he put them in a ready-made pie shell he found in his freezer. He dotted the apples with butter and covered them with the top crust. He put the pie in the oven and baked it for ten minutes. Andy reduced the heat to 350° and continued baking the pie for another 40 minutes. When he finally took the pie out of the oven, it looked perfect to serve to his company later.

1. Why was Andy making an apple pie?

2. What temperature did he preheat the oven to?

3. How many cups of apples did he slice?

4. What spices did he use in the pie?

5. What kind of pie shell did Andy use?

6. What did Andy do just before he put on the top crust?

7. How long did the pie bake at 450°?

8. What did he reduce the temperature to?

9. How much longer did the pie bake at 350°?

10. Who was going to eat the pie?

Home Maintenance Activities

The activities in the second half of this book address general knowledge associated with home maintenance. Much of the content should be familiar to your client, although the format of some of the tasks is very specific and will only be familiar to the client who has engaged in the activity associated with the specific item. For example, almost all of your clients will know something about painting, but not all will know that a primer coat of paint is needed on a wall previously painted with an oil-based paint. Thus, at times, you will need to ascertain if a task is appropriate for a client based on his previous experiences and knowledge base.

The familiar and relevant content will increase your client's interest as it taps into information stored in his remote memory. This will make your client feel like the tasks apply directly to him. These tasks are designed to utilize your client's foundational skills to improve language and cognitive processing, sentence formulation, and verbal expression.

Word Finding

Everyone has some degree of word-finding difficulty, but for someone who has a brain dysfunction, the frequency of anomic difficulties is intensified. A client will frequently attempt to rationalize that he cannot remember a word because it is not familiar to him. However, the familiarity of content in these tasks will increase your client's awareness that he indeed has difficulty with word finding and will encourage him to remediate the problem.

The tasks in this section address several layers of naming skills, including the following.

- confrontational naming
- making associations
- matching words to definitions
- naming objects from descriptions
- naming whole objects when given a part
- comparing items to determine which fit a superlative condition
- listing items from tasks

The tasks target word finding related to tools, making home repairs, home maintenance chores, painting, plumbing, carpentry, and electrical work.

Naming Pictures

Name these pictures.

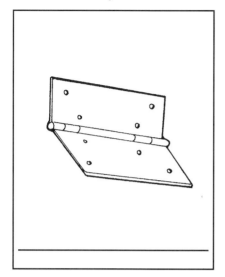
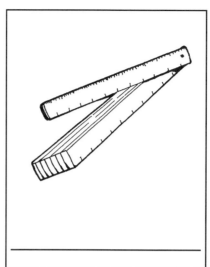
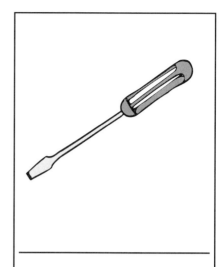

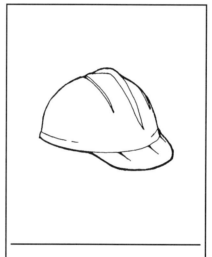
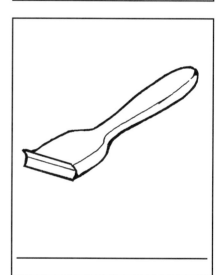
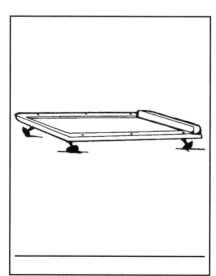
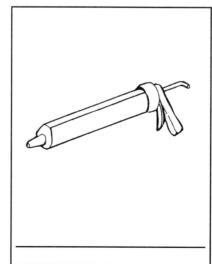
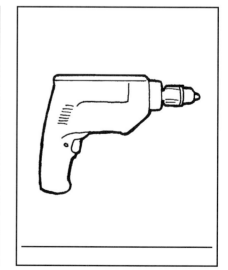

Naming Pictures

Name these pictures.

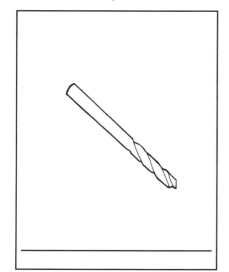

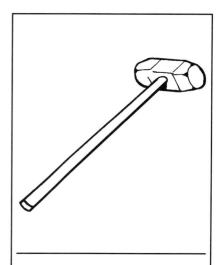
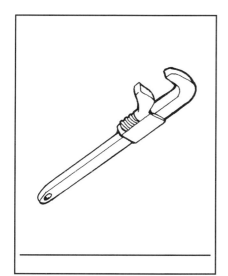
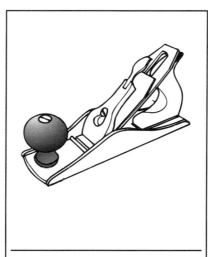
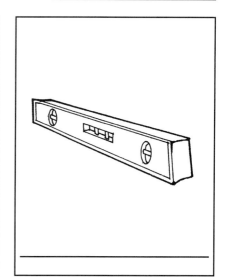
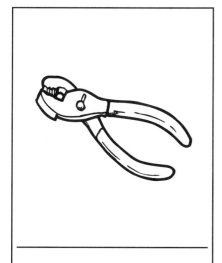
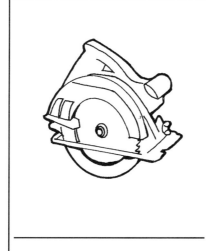
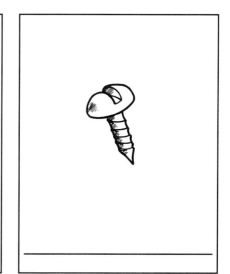

Naming Pictures

Name these pictures.

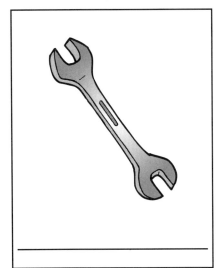
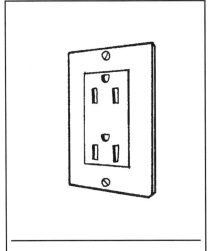
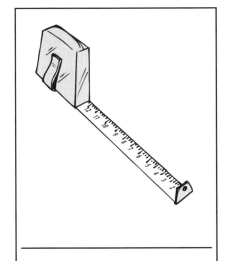
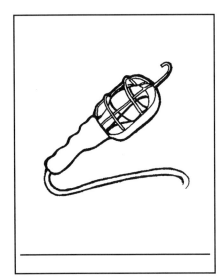
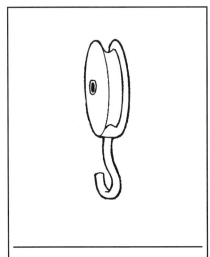
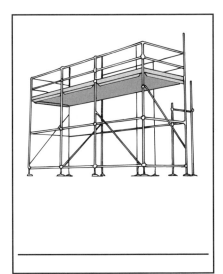
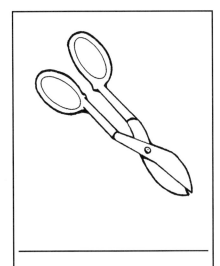
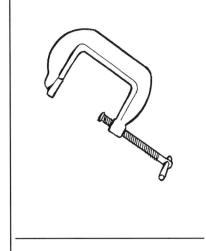
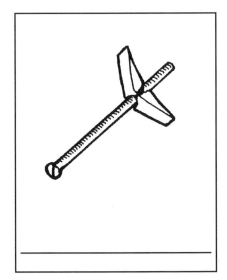

Matching Words to Pictures

Find a word to match each picture. Draw a line from the word to the picture.

thermometer

scaffold

hard hat

stepladder

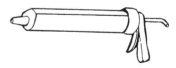

caulking gun

Matching Words to Pictures

Find a word to match each picture. Draw a line from the word to the picture.

ballpeen hammer

extension light

pulley

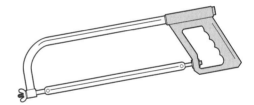

hacksaw

tin snips

Matching Words to Pictures

Find a word to match each picture. Draw a line from the word to the picture.

cordless drill

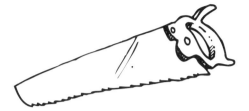

screwdriver

handsaw

putty knife

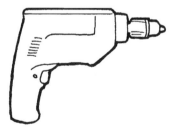

wrench

Making Associations

Find a word on the left that goes with a word in the box. The first one is done for you.

Left	Box
counter ————————————————	hammer
circuit	———— sink
claw	nut
dry	wall
hardware	drill
caulking	bolt
wing	iron
rain	breaker
sump	wood
soldering	gun
extension	cord
pressure-treated	tack
toggle	gutter
thumb	store
cordless	pump

Home Maintenance Activities—Word Finding
WALC 11: Language for Home Activities

Making Associations

Find a word on the left that goes with a word in the box. The first one is done for you.

machine	jamb
putty	mower
sand	blade
smoke	hole
ballpeen	screw
tin	brush
pilot	detector
door	paper
screw	hammer
lawn	ladder
step	tools
power	driver
paint	trimmer
saw	knife
hedge	snips

machine is connected to *screw*.

Making Associations

Find a word on the left that goes with a word in the box. The first one is done for you.

monkey	roller
latex	tile
snow	blower
sledge	screwdriver
needlenose	wrench
paint	hammer
duct	snake
fiberglass	tape
Venetian	plug
3-prong	blinds
Phillips head	pliers
chain	saw
plumber's	gun
ceramic	insulation
staple	paint

monkey is connected to wrench.

Matching Words to Definitions

Match each word to its definition. Write the letter on the blank.

1. _____ asphalt
2. _____ circuit breaker
3. _____ hammer
4. _____ handle
5. _____ epoxy
6. _____ cement
7. _____ outlet
8. _____ hook
9. _____ sash
10. _____ saw
11. _____ roof
12. _____ dowel

a. a tool used for driving in nails

b. a strong glue

c. a tool used to cut wood

d. a curved piece of wire or plastic for hanging things on

e. a part of a window

f. material used in making sidewalks

g. it trips when an outlet is overloaded

h. a black, sticky substance used in paving roads

i. used for carrying something

j. a round wooden peg used to join two pieces of wood

k. a fixture into which a cord is plugged

l. it covers a house

Matching Words to Definitions

Match each word to its definition. Write the letter on the blank.

1. _____ plumber's snake
2. _____ current
3. _____ padlock
4. _____ joint
5. _____ veneer
6. _____ vent
7. _____ hardwood
8. _____ awl
9. _____ stain
10. _____ screw
11. _____ washer
12. _____ snow blower

a. the place where wood or pipes join

b. a small plastic, metal, or rubber ring

c. used to darken wood

d. an auger used for unclogging drains

e. a metal fastener with threads

f. a pointed tool used to make holes

g. a thin layer of wood

h. used to secure gates, bikes, etc.

i. clears the sidewalk of winter weather

j. a flow of electrical charge

k. an outlet for air, smoke, or fumes

l. used for flooring

Matching Words to Definitions

Match each word to its definition. Write the letter on the blank.

1. _____ toggle bolt

2. _____ paint

3. _____ level

4. _____ spackle

5. _____ scaffold

6. _____ post

7. _____ canvas

8. _____ thermostat

9. _____ notch

10. _____ pipe

11. _____ extension cord

12. _____ pliers

a. used to determine if an object is straight

b. a temporary platform for workers

c. a device used for regulating temperature

d. the upright part of a fence

e. a strong, rough, cloth material

f. a wing nut that opens up behind a wall

g. a V-shaped cut in a surface

h. used to fill small holes or cracks in walls

i. used to cover or color walls

j. used when a tool's cord is too short

k. a tool used for gripping and bending

l. a metal or polyurethane tube that water flows through

Naming Objects from Descriptions

What object is described?

1. This is used to cut wood. _____

2. This is a material used to build a retaining wall. _____

3. This is a material used in fencing. _____

4. This is something used by a carpenter. _____

5. This tool is used for turning screws. _____

6. This material is used in making sidewalks. _____

7. This professional fixes water problems. _____

8. This is a type of kitchen flooring. _____

9. This is used to coat wood. _____

10. This is used around bathtub seams. _____

11. This provides light on a work area. _____

12. This is used to dig a hole. _____

13. This worker designs and cares for lawns. _____

14. This is used to unclog a drain. _____

15. This is used to clean paintbrushes. _____

Naming Objects from Descriptions

What object is described?

1. This tool is used to pound in nails. _____

2. This is used to change channels from the sofa. _____

3. This is something used by an electrician. _____

4. This is put on lawns and gardens. _____

5. This is put on floors. _____

6. This is used to trim around lawn edges. _____

7. This is used to remove snow from walks. _____

8. This professional replaces a roof. _____

9. This device is used for holding items firmly. _____

10. This takes the moisture out of the air. _____

11. This is put between bricks and stones. _____

12. This is used to adjust the temperature of the air. _____

13. This room contains tools and a workbench. _____

14. This rough paper is used to smooth wood. _____

15. This is used to start a barbecue grill. _____

Naming Objects from Descriptions

What object is described?

1. This is used to cut the grass. _____

2. This cools the air in the hot summer. _____

3. This professional designs buildings. _____

4. This is where one can park a car. _____

5. This is an enclosure on the back of a house. _____

6. This tool is used to make holes in wood. _____

7. This material is used to make furniture. _____

8. This is something used by a plumber. _____

9. This runs along the roof's edge to carry away rainwater. _____

10. This is used to clean up leaves. _____

11. This is used to repair cracks in walls. _____

12. This is a material used for building houses. _____

13. This melts the ice off walks in the winter. _____

14. This measures temperature. _____

15. This is climbed on to reach high places. _____

Naming Wholes from Parts

Name an object associated with each part.

1. shingles _____
2. nails _____
3. hinge _____
4. rungs _____
5. teeth _____
6. bricks _____
7. prongs _____
8. numbers _____
9. beam _____
10. bristles _____
11. battery _____
12. threads _____
13. lid _____
14. slats _____
15. drain _____
16. handle _____
17. jaws _____
18. cord _____
19. blade _____
20. motor _____
21. plug _____
22. rafter _____
23. joint _____
24. flue _____
25. gears _____
26. cement _____
27. head _____
28. washer _____
29. gutters _____
30. nozzle _____

Naming Wholes from Parts

Name an object associated with each part.

1. keyhole _____
2. gas _____
3. vent _____
4. showerhead _____
5. burner _____
6. stone _____
7. putty _____
8. tube _____
9. frame _____
10. railing _____
11. brush _____
12. engine _____
13. switch _____
14. tile _____
15. pane _____
16. plate _____
17. steps _____
18. faucet _____
19. floor _____
20. plank _____
21. jack _____
22. sand _____
23. drawer _____
24. thermostat _____
25. latch _____
26. screen _____
27. speaker _____
28. hose _____
29. chain _____
30. door _____

Comparing Items

Circle the answer.

Which item is the _____

1.	**longest?**	inch	yard	foot
2.	**lightest?**	screw	brick	saw
3.	**darkest?**	white	black	beige
4.	**strongest?**	twine	string	rope
5.	**tallest?**	garage	house	shed
6.	**hottest?**	soldering iron	nail	pliers
7.	**widest?**	shack	trailer	mansion
8.	**loudest?**	siren	alarm clock	television
9.	**hardest?**	putty	stone	grout
10.	**longest?**	yard	meter	mile
11.	**sharpest?**	putty knife	penknife	level
12.	**heaviest?**	handsaw	hacksaw	chain saw
13.	**wettest?**	paint	sandpaper	caulking
14.	**weakest?**	duct tape	masking tape	metal bar
15.	**shortest?**	hour	minute	second

Comparing Items

Circle the answer.

Which item is the _____

1.	**shortest?**	yard	inch	mile
2.	**heaviest?**	plywood	nail	beam
3.	**hardest?**	clay	steel	dirt
4.	**brightest?**	spotlight	lamp	flashlight
5.	**driest?**	thinner	drywall	turpentine
6.	**smoothest?**	concrete	sandpaper	glass
7.	**coldest?**	plaster	dry ice	cement
8.	**tallest?**	tree	bush	shrub
9.	**roughest?**	sandpaper	paint	plaster
10.	**quietest?**	horn	siren	beep
11.	**blackest?**	tar	cement	plaster
12.	**lightest?**	mallet	tape rule	sledgehammer
13.	**largest?**	lawn mower	shovel	backhoe
14.	**thinnest?**	beam	plywood	rafter
15.	**sharpest?**	wrench	pliers	saw

Listing Items for Tasks

List four things you need for each activity.

Taking Care of a Lawn

1. _____ 3. _____

2. _____ 4. _____

Painting a Room

1. _____ 3. _____

2. _____ 4. _____

Building Bookshelves

1. _____ 3. _____

2. _____ 4. _____

Barbecueing

1. _____ 3. _____

2. _____ 4. _____

Listing Items for Tasks

List four things you need for each job.

Repairing a Crack in the Wall

1. _____ 3. _____

2. _____ 4. _____

Fixing a Wooden Porch Step

1. _____ 3. _____

2. _____ 4. _____

Hanging a Picture

1. _____ 3. _____

2. _____ 4. _____

Maintaining a Car

1. _____ 3. _____

2. _____ 4. _____

Organization

The tasks in this section involve organization of thoughts. Being able to think in a logical, organized manner will improve your client's ability to take information and comprehend it in a hierarchical manner. This will help negate the tendency to think divergently or to utilize mental manipulation in a manner that becomes tangential and off course. The tasks are organized as follows to stimulate this progression in thinking to achieve a desired goal.

- In tasks where your client unscrambles words, he first needs to recall word possibilities within the category and make an organized decision for which word is the correct item. Then he needs to order the letters correctly to form the word.

- When unscrambling words to make a sentence related to tools and repairs, completing paragraphs related to common household problems, or sequencing the steps of home repair activities, your client must use the content in an organized, progressive manner.

- When completing the scheduling activities, your client must use the information presented in the paragraph and organize it based on content and on time sequence.

The content of the tasks in this section focuses on carpentry, tools, electricity, household chores, and home repair.

Unscrambling Words

Unscramble each word. The first letter is capitalized and underlined.

Carpentry Words

1. a <u>S</u> w
2. o <u>W</u> d o
3. i a <u>S</u> n t
4. o n t i <u>J</u>
5. <u>V</u> n a s r i h
6. l p <u>C</u> a m
7. o e w l <u>D</u>
8. n <u>B</u> o d
9. e v <u>B</u> l e
10. <u>W</u> d g e e

Tool Words

1. h e <u>C</u> s i l
2. w r o l <u>T</u> e
3. l r i <u>D</u> l
4. m <u>H</u> m a e r
5. l e <u>L</u> v e
6. e l a <u>P</u> n
7. e l i <u>P</u> r s
8. r d v c r r w i <u>S</u> e e
9. n <u>T</u> i n s <u>S</u> i p
10. e r n h c <u>W</u>

Unscrambling Words

Unscramble each word. The first letter is capitalized and underlined.

Electricity Words

1. t t W a
2. u e s F
3. h S k c o
4. o r C d
5. r o e w P
6. p k r S a
7. l g P u
8. r i W e
9. m s p A
10. h w t i S c

Home Repair Words

1. a t n P i
2. u C l k a
3. u r t o G
4. n S a d
5. l e u G
6. i O l
7. h s o l P i
8. a S t n i
9. r c a S e p
10. i h t T e g n

Unscrambling Words

Unscramble each word. The first letter is capitalized and underlined.

Wallpapering Words

1. r e a <u>W</u> t
2. l <u>W</u> l a
3. a e <u>P</u> r p
4. p <u>S</u> r t i s
5. d r a e d <u>L</u>
6. s o <u>R</u> l l
7. m <u>S</u> a e
8. a r t t e <u>P</u> n
9. <u>B</u> s u h r
10. n f <u>K</u> i e

Home Appliances

1. e o <u>S</u> v t
2. n a <u>C</u>   p e <u>O</u> n r e
3. o c l <u>C</u> k   a <u>R</u> i d o
4. w i <u>M</u> a v c o r e
5. e f <u>C</u> o f e k m a r e
6. t <u>T</u> s a e o r
7. h <u>W</u> e s a r
8. o r g f <u>R</u> a e i e r t r
9. w e r <u>D</u> s h a i h s
10. y r <u>D</u> r e

Unscrambling Sentences

Unscramble each sentence. The first word in the sentence is capitalized.

1. rule A used is tape measuring for.
   _____

2. used is paving Asphalt in mixtures.
   _____

3. wing A sides has nut flared.
   _____

4. excess sump away drains pump A water.
   _____

5. Stain to used wood is color.
   _____

6. glass careful broken Be handling when.
   _____

7. are of porcelain out Most made toilets.
   _____

8. disposable Do bags reuse vacuum not.
   _____

9. latches by doors held are closed Cupboard.
   _____

10. help A can washer fix leaky a faucet.
    _____

Unscrambling Sentences

Unscramble each sentence. The first word in the sentence is capitalized.

1. the Is out lightbulb?
   _____

2. tightening a nut wrench Try the with.
   _____

3. ladder level a ground firm on Place.
   _____

4. garbage not in glass Do your disposal grind.
   _____

5. dresser on A slides runners drawer.
   _____

6. is close used holes Sealer to.
   _____

7. of layers Plywood veneer of is made.
   _____

8. parts is to used join Solder metal.
   _____

9. can bolts used hang to be Toggle pictures.
   _____

10. and go air chimney Smoke a up hot.
    _____

Unscrambling Sentences

Unscramble each sentence. The first word in the sentence is capitalized.

1. are aluminum Many covered siding homes in.
   _____

2. basement workshop the in can located A be.
   _____

3. sawhorses cutting on Support when planks.
   _____

4. cleanup and a brush for Use dustpan.
   _____

5. smooth is wood to Sandpaper used.
   _____

6. Spray hinges lubricating squeaky compound a with.
   _____

7. fire smoke against warns A detector.
   _____

8. a can Paint appear on blisters wall.
   _____

9. the breaker go circuit lights If check the out.
   _____

10. choose usually for repairs screws Carpenters.
    _____

Completing a Paragraph

Use the words in the box to fill in the blanks.

brush	ease	with	rusty
never	condition	soot	expert
flashlight	closed	damper	

Fireplace Damper Won't Open or Close Easily

The metal may be corroded or caked with _____. Shine a _____ on the damper to check its _____. If the damper is _____ and encrusted _____ soot, use a wire _____ to clean the soot and rust off. Then try moving the _____ until it works with _____. If you can't move the damper, call an _____ to do the job. Warning: _____ light a fire when the damper is stuck _____!

Completing a Paragraph

Use the words in the box to fill in the blanks.

expensive	cook	removing	size
solve	everything	space	large
another	kitchen	steps	

Making Space in a Kitchen

One common _____ problem in a home is a small, cramped _____. Enlarging the kitchen, however, may not _____ the problem. In fact, a kitchen may be too _____ to be efficient and could overwork the _____ because too many _____ are needed to get from one work area to _____. Instead of _____ a wall to increase the _____ of the kitchen, consider some less _____ and easier changes that will make better use of the space you have and keep _____ you need within reach.

Completing a Paragraph

Use the words in the box to fill in the blanks.

circuit	tripped	plug	fix
electric	electrician	loose	lamp
outlet	fails	frayed	

Why Won't This Heater Work?

If your _____ heater won't turn on, you should first examine the cord and _____. If the cord is _____ around the plug, the plug is broken, or the prongs are _____, you should replace the plug. If this isn't the problem, then check the _____ breaker to see if it has _____. If none of these problems exist, check the wall _____ with a _____ that works. If the lamp _____ to turn on, you can be sure the wall outlet isn't working and it's time to call the _____ because you need a professional to _____ the problem.

Completing a Paragraph

Use the words in the box to fill in the blanks.

hold	material	rivets	flatten
hole	place	petals	tool
end	through	spread	

Installing Rivets

Various types of _____ are used to join metal pieces and wood. To install a rivet, drill a small _____ the same size as the rivet in each piece of the _____ you will be joining. Insert the rivet _____ these holes. Next, hammer the tail _____ of the rivet so the edges _____ out and catch the surface of the material. Finally, set the scored end with a riveting _____. The scored sections will _____ out so they look like the _____ of a flower. These petals _____ the rivet and joined material in _____.

Sequencing

Put the following steps in the correct order by numbering them. Then, name the task.

Set A _____

_____ Pump up and down vigorously several times.
_____ Get out the plunger.
_____ Check to see if water will go down the drain.
_____ Notice the kitchen drain seems clogged.
_____ Put the plunger over the drain opening.

Set B _____

_____ Put the mower away.
_____ Walk out to the shed.
_____ Fill the mower with gas.
_____ Mow the lawn.
_____ Get the mower from the shed.

Set C _____

_____ Hammer a picture hanger on the spot.
_____ Make sure the picture is hanging straight.
_____ Mark a spot on the wall.
_____ Hang the picture on the hanger.
_____ Choose a picture to hang.

Set D _____

_____ Wipe the wall with a damp cloth.
_____ Move furniture away from the wall.
_____ Put down a drop cloth.
_____ Clean up.
_____ Paint the wall.

Sequencing

Put the following steps in the correct order by numbering them. Then, name the task.

Set A _____

_____ Rinse the pieces and dry thoroughly.
_____ Exert pressure on the mend.
_____ Bring the pieces together so they are interlocked.
_____ Clean the plate's broken edges with a mild detergent.
_____ Leave the plate in place until the glue dries.
_____ Apply a thin coating of glue along both edges.

Set B _____

_____ Take the plank's measurements.
_____ Pry out the rotten plank.
_____ Nail the new plank in place.
_____ Buy a replacement plank.
_____ Cover the space so someone doesn't fall in.
_____ Coat the new plank with preservative.

Set C _____

_____ Prepare the soil.
_____ Weed when necessary.
_____ Plant the seedlings.
_____ Pick the vegetables.
_____ Decide where you want the vegetable garden.
_____ Water the seedlings.

Set D _____

_____ Polish when the wax dries.
_____ Wash the car.
_____ Wipe off any spots missed.
_____ Let the water dry off the car.
_____ Rinse the car.
_____ Apply wax.

Sequencing

Put the following sentences in the correct order by numbering them. Then, name the task.

Set A _____

_____ After you put the pins in the sockets, turn the tube ¼ of the way around to make it fit snug.

_____ A fluorescent bulb is held in the light fixture by pins at either end of the tube that are pushed into the sockets.

_____ If the light flickers, try turning the tube to make the connection better.

Set B _____

_____ This will make the door slide easily.

_____ Coat the bottom and sides of the metal track with a silicone lubricating compound.

_____ With the door completely open, clean out the track along the floor.

Set C _____

_____ It can be very frustrating to get caught in a room because the doorknob came off in your hand.

_____ Use a screwdriver to tighten the screws that hold the knob in place.

_____ To prevent this, you will want to fix it right away instead of waiting.

Set D _____

_____ To prevent the clips from getting loose, use the correct fasteners.

_____ Use toggle bolts to secure the clips on a hollow wall.

_____ If the wall is solid, the mirror will need expansion fasteners and screws.

_____ An unframed mirror should be mounted with clips along the top, bottom, and sides.

Completing a Schedule

Use the clues to fill in the schedule.

> You have three major tasks to complete this weekend—caulking the tub, painting your bedroom, and wallpapering the bathroom. You want to watch your favorite team play football. List the steps you need to follow so you finish the tasks before the game begins.
>
> You know you'll need supplies from the hardware store, so first you **check what you have at home** and then **make a list** of what you need. When you get home from the **hardware store**, you **paint the bedroom** and quickly **clean up** the drop cloths, brushes, rollers, paints, and pans. Then, it's on to **wallpapering the bathroom**. Before you wallpaper, you **wash down the walls**. While the paper is drying, you **caulk the bathtub**. You **clean up the bathroom** just as the pregame show ends. By now, you're ready for the **game and a nap**!

1st _____

2nd _____

3rd _____

4th _____

5th _____

6th _____

7th _____

8th _____

9th _____

Last _____

Completing a Schedule

Use the clues to fill in the schedule.

> John needs to plan his morning. He needs to finish his errands by noon so he can pick up a lumber order at the **home improvement center**. John plans to get up at 8:00, **shower, and eat breakfast** so he can be out of the house by 8:45.
>
> John knows he has to stop at the **bank** to get some money after he gets gas. The **hardware store** and **gas station** don't open until 10:00. Since the **hardware store** is next to the home improvement center, John will go to the hardware store on his way to the home improvement center.
>
> The **post office** and **Farm and Family Center** are closest to John's house and they are open the earliest. There is usually a line at the post office by 9:30, so he plans to be there before then. He wants to be at the gas station when it opens. He plans on being at the **AutoStore** at 11:00.

8:00 _____

9:00 _____

9:30 _____

10:00 _____

10:30 _____

11:00 _____

11:30 _____

12:00 _____

Categorization

Information is stored in the brain in a highly organized, logical manner. One of the systems we use for storage and retrieval is categorization. The tasks in this section will help your client reestablish categorizing strategies.

- Tasks that involve listing items needed to complete familiar activities will assist in recall of multiple words.

- Tasks that require your client to locate five words related to a given category provide the information as to how many words he must find. That information is not present in the next task where your client must locate multiple items that belong to a category without knowing exactly how many to find. This encourages language and cognitive processing and flexible thinking as your client determines which words belong to the given category.

- When naming the category, your client must use the categorizing skill in reverse order to determine how the task items are related.

The content of the tasks in this section focuses on tools, hardware, painting, and building materials.

Categorizing — Listing Items

List as many items as you can for each category.

Hand Tools

1. _____
2. _____
3. _____
4. _____
5. _____
6. _____
7. _____
8. _____

Things Used by a Plumber

1. _____
2. _____
3. _____
4. _____
5. _____
6. _____
7. _____
8. _____

Parts of a Car

1. _____
2. _____
3. _____
4. _____
5. _____
6. _____
7. _____
8. _____

Categorizing — Listing Items

List as many items as you can for each category.

Tools and Things that Cut

1. _____ 5. _____
2. _____ 6. _____
3. _____ 7. _____
4. _____ 8. _____

Things in a Toolbox

1. _____ 5. _____
2. _____ 6. _____
3. _____ 7. _____
4. _____ 8. _____

Garden and Lawn Care Items

1. _____ 5. _____
2. _____ 6. _____
3. _____ 7. _____
4. _____ 8. _____

Categorizing — Listing Items

List as many items as you can for each category.

Occupations Involved in Construction

1. _____
2. _____
3. _____
4. _____
5. _____
6. _____
7. _____
8. _____

Things in a Hardware Store

1. _____
2. _____
3. _____
4. _____
5. _____
6. _____
7. _____
8. _____

Things Used by an Electrician

1. _____
2. _____
3. _____
4. _____
5. _____
6. _____
7. _____
8. _____

Categorizing — Selecting 5 Items

Identify five words in each box associated with the word on the left.

Hammer	ballpeen skin	flake head	claw nails	handle water
Lawn	claim mower	fertilizer rye grass	edging truck	sale crabgrass
Toolbox	stairs lid	tools drama	reason latch	handle carry
Attic	rafters hot	furnace beams	roof mower	storage report
Car	fender tracks	dipstick radiator	cockpit muffler	caboose battery
Carpentry	asphalt wood	nails tires	sanding hammer	cupboards snake

Categorizing — Selecting 5 Items

Identify five words in each box associated with the word on the left.

Building Materials	brick　　water　　stone　　hose wood　　cement　　soil　　concrete

Electricity	watts　　wires　　weeds　　amps tiles　　current　　cord　　flue

Hardware	grain　　hinges　　screws　　glue nails　　panel　　washers　　bolts

Woods	daisy　　bread　　cherry　　mahogany oak　　pine　　rye　　walnut

Tools	chisel　　wrench　　rope　　pliers hammer　　bucket　　punch　　porch

Painting	roller　　thinner　　brush　　drop cloth hair　　paint　　shoe　　chew

Categorizing — Selecting Correct Items

Identify the items that belong in each category.

Electrical Words	switch	outlet	watts
	saw	seats	whistle
	circuit	current	wire
	volts	shower	asphalt

Metals	wallpaper	tape	aluminum
	iron	steel	plastic
	gold	tin	rubber
	brass	copper	silver

Things that Cut	razor	plane	box cutter
	tin snips	helmet	wiper
	level	jigsaw	shears
	tape measure	hacksaw	can

Parts of a Truck	shorts	suspension	dark
	exhaust	spiral	windows
	engine	web	hail
	windshield	bed	roof

Measurements	zipper	yard	pound
	inch	ton	phone
	brick	ranch	mile
	meter	foot	ounce

Categorizing — Selecting Correct Items

Identify the items that belong in each category.

Painting Words	roller	saw	drips
	primer	drop cloth	drill
	aluminum	brush	latex
	carpet	salt	thinner

Plumbing Words	watch	pipes	healing
	water	sting	sink
	faucet	acre	chimney
	drains	toilet	shower

Tools	saw	pliers	chisel
	oil	trucker	hammer
	punch	wrench	awl
	plane	boots	estimate

Parts of a House	hallway	walls	series
	bedroom	hatch	basement
	cloud	watch	roof
	stairs	kitchen	bathroom

Carpentry Words	nails	wood	path
	lathe	plane	boards
	pillow	pipes	strainer
	caulking	sander	varnish

Categorizing — Selecting Correct Items

Identify the items that belong in each category.

Laborers and Workers	plumber roofer flower painter	lounger mason sleeper contractor	wafer electrician landscaper fortune
Lawn Care	fertilizer taping watering rice	weed killer edging mowing flicking	flour seeding flushing trimming
Things in a Garage	staple shovel broom shelves	dynamite rake stairway car	flowerpots hoe bucket milk
Building Materials	suds cement stone brick	concrete juice steel dust	iron wood tile ashes
Cleaning Items	shop vac trunk night dustpan	girder rags vacuum pliers	broom twine mop towels

Naming the Category

Name the category for each list of items.

1. folding rule, tape measure, ruler, yardstick _____

2. latex, semi-gloss, enamel, primer _____

3. carpenter, architect, plumber, roofer _____

4. nail, bolt, washer, screw _____

5. varnish, shellac, paint, stain _____

6. wrench, hammer, chisel, pliers _____

7. building supply, hardware store, lumberyard _____

8. iron, brass, steel, copper _____

9. paint tray, brushes, rollers, drop cloth _____

10. rake, hoe, trowel, shovel _____

11. oak, pine, walnut, cherry _____

12. inch, yard, meter, foot _____

13. wood, stone, cement, concrete _____

14. hack, circular, hand, coping _____

15. scissors, tin snips, saw, razor _____

Naming the Category

Name the category for each list of items.

1. basement, rooms, attic, roof _____

2. hornets, carpenter ants, termites, silverfish _____

3. jar, can, box, bag _____

4. mallet, sledge, ballpeen, tack _____

5. Phillips head, flat head _____

6. brick, boards, steel, plaster _____

7. fertilizer, seed, weed killer, grub control _____

8. beam, girder, joist, rafter _____

9. dustpan, broom, brush, rags _____

10. flathead, machine, masonry, wood _____

11. circuit, current, flow, wires _____

12. pipe wrench, snake, plunger, blow torch _____

13. oil, grease, WD-40, petroleum jelly _____

14. Allen, monkey, pipe, adjustable _____

15. goggles, helmet, steel-toed boots _____

Naming the Category

Name the category for each list of items.

1. step, extension, aluminum, straight _____

2. flagstone, slate, granite, mica _____

3. plasterboard, plywood, paneling, drywall _____

4. paintings, portraits, tapestries, mirrors _____

5. mortar hoe, trowel, edger, jointer _____

6. heat pump, boiler, furnace, radiator _____

7. varnish, shellac, polyurethane _____

8. vise, clamp, screws, jig _____

9. hardwood, tile, linoleum, carpet _____

10. height, weight, length, width _____

11. rust, mildew, decay, dry rot _____

12. rope, twine, string, thread _____

13. yew, boxwood, arborvitae, privet _____

14. common, finishing, masonry, ten-penny _____

15. adhesive, epoxy, rubber cement, acrylic resin _____

Reasoning

The tasks in this section involve the skill of being able to use salient information to deduce an answer. To encourage thought flexibility as well as to discourage fixation, items within a task are not always uniform (e.g., some questions require a specific answer while others may have more than one right answer).

- When making word deductions, your client must reason how the words relate and utilize convergent reasoning to determine the answer.

- For category exclusion, your client must be able to compare and contrast multiple words to deduce which of the words does not belong with the others.

- Sentence and picture analogies involve deducing how the first pair of items are related and then carrying over that process so it is reflected in the second set of items.

- Identifying and then correcting incongruities in sentences involves verbal reasoning based on knowledge stored in your client's memory. Many of the sentences can be corrected in multiple ways, so it will require your client to make a determination as to which correction is best suited for the item according to his knowledge base.

- When determining if sentences are true or false, your client must be able to read the sentence, compare it to his knowledge, and then determine its correctness.

- For tasks involving comparing sentences to determine if they mean the same thing, your client needs to ascertain if word order affects the meaning or if the content in one sentence means the same as the other sentence. He must then make a determination based on grammar, word order, and content.

- The tasks for evaluating information incorporate a unique format in that they are more subjective. The items address things your client would or would not do depending upon his knowledge and background. This allows your client to have more freedom in his responses as they are based on his own personal preferences.

- The deductive reasoning tasks give practice using clues to determine which item fits the given content. They also incorporate an exclusion principle as it is easier to determine the answer by eliminating all unrelated items.

The content of the tasks in this section focuses on home and garden tools and equipment and home repair.

Making Word Deductions

What item is described by the clue words?

1. rough, paper, smooth, wood _____

2. tool, turns, screws, handle _____

3. privacy, posts, surround, gate _____

4. two prongs, electrical, cord _____

5. hardware, attaches door, frame _____

6. cut, sharp, handle, blades _____

7. bristles, handle, nylon, spreads paint _____

8. primer, latex, high-gloss, flat _____

9. hit, handle, claw, nails _____

10. shingles, slope, gutters, ridge _____

11. flue, damper, smoke, fire brick _____

12. faucet, basin, handles, drain _____

13. clear, furniture, coating, protection _____

14. handle, monkey, grasps, adjustable _____

15. fenders, engine, roof, drive _____

Making Word Deductions

What item is described by the clue words?

1. long, electricity, wire, plug _____

2. blades, air, circulates, cools _____

3. glass, socket, lamp, bright _____

4. one wheel, garden, handles, push _____

5. pointed, head, hammer, metal _____

6. blade, cut, teeth, handle _____

7. climb, rungs, extension, height _____

8. vegetables, plot, weeds, water _____

9. laces, feet, steel-toed, protection _____

10. adjust, heater, temperature, degrees _____

11. bristles, cleaning, sweep, handle _____

12. grass, cut, gasoline, motor _____

13. metal-eater, corrosion, cars _____

14. turns, door, grasp, locks _____

15. handle, turns, bores holes _____

Making Word Deductions

What item is described by the clue words?

1. degrees, mercury, temperature, measures _____

2. head protection, hard, brim _____

3. C-shaped, tightens, holds _____

4. white, patches cracks, walls _____

5. tool, beveled edge, shaves wood _____

6. handle, bladed head, chops _____

7. black, paving, sticky, hard _____

8. heavy material, awnings, tents, sail _____

9. silver, roll, sticky, holds _____

10. unclogs, rubber cup, handle, suction _____

11. hang, strips, pattern, seams _____

12. weigh, balanced, gauge, pounds _____

13. container, liquid, handle, carry _____

14. blade, handle, cut, sharp _____

15. straight, used for measuring, inches _____

Determining Category Exclusions

Mark the word that does not belong with the others.

1.	mallet	curved claw	wrench	sledge
2.	welder	cook	plumber	painter
3.	varnish	stain	paint	glass
4.	rafters	sink	shower	toilet
5.	adjustable	monkey	nail	allen
6.	damper	scraper	sandpaper	putty knife
7.	boards	beams	pipes	planks
8.	circuit	flow	current	paper
9.	pipe	brick	hose	tube
10.	sandpaper	screws	bolts	nails
11.	dustpan	broom	vacuum	card
12.	grout	plaster	can	spackle
13.	beam	glue	epoxy	paste
14.	stones	block	brick	oil
15.	plans	pole	designs	blueprints

Determining Category Exclusions

Mark the word that does not belong with the others.

1. roll — nut — washer — bolt
2. plane — chisel — lathe — linoleum
3. pine — rose — oak — cherry
4. faucet — basin — pipes — shed
5. chain saw — hacksaw — seesaw — handsaw
6. plank — spackle — plastic wood — putty
7. gutter — rain spout — wheel — downspout
8. stove — train — freezer — oven
9. can — jar — box — sieve
10. pool — shovel — hoe — rake
11. glass — ceramic — steel — porcelain
12. paper — bubble — blister — peel
13. cut — slice — slit — age
14. wobbly — firm — shaky — unstable
15. duct tape — masking tape — tape worm — electrical tape

Completing Picture Analogies

Circle the picture on the right that solves each analogy.

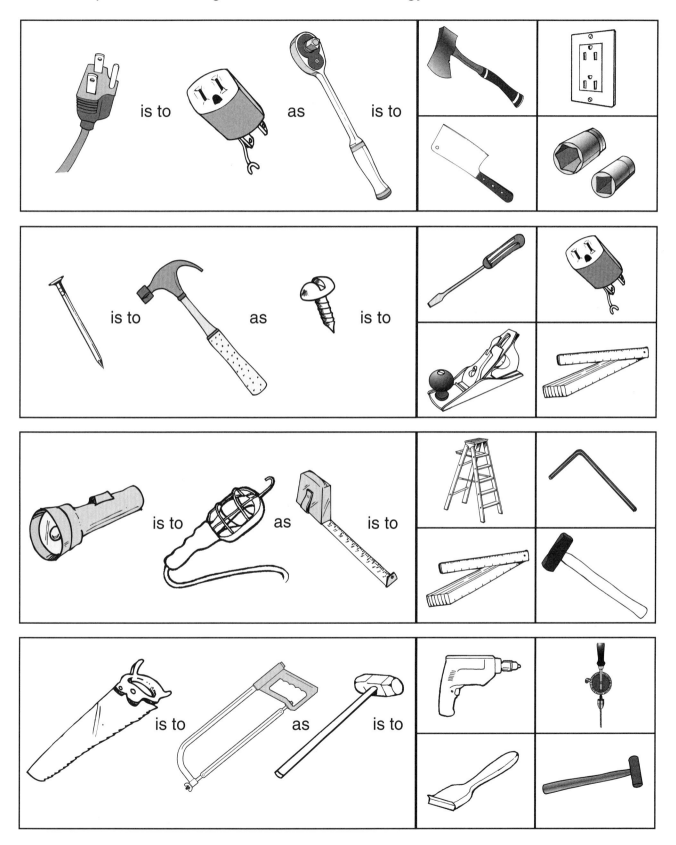

Completing Picture Analogies

Circle the picture on the right that solves each analogy.

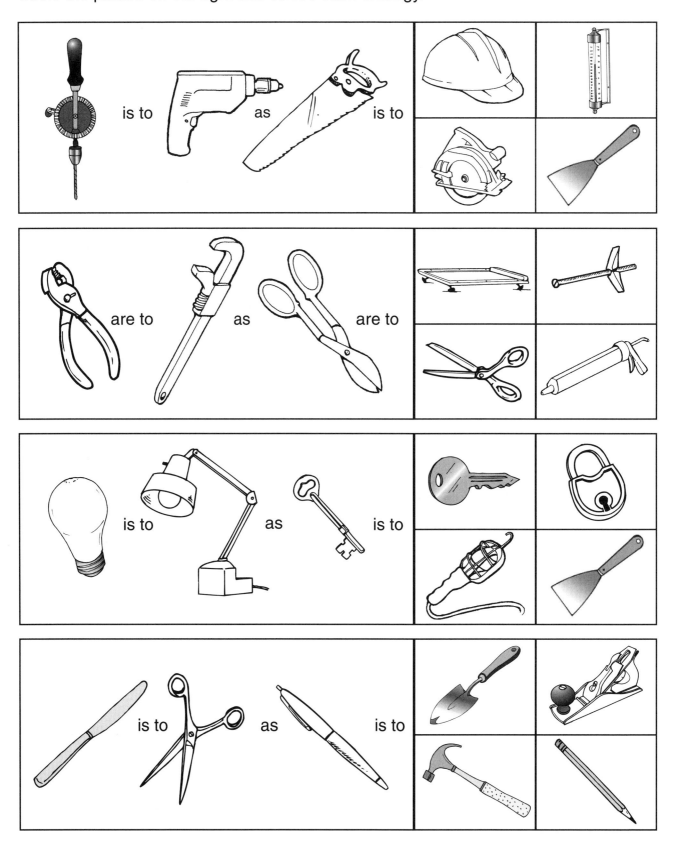

Completing Sentence Analogies

Complete the analogies.

1. A rug is put on the floor; paint is put on the _____.

2. A vise grasps; a hammer _____.

3. A saw has teeth; a brush has _____.

4. Solder is made of metal; windows are made of _____.

5. Paint is used to cover; glue is used to _____.

6. *Rim* means the same as *edge*; *portion* means the same as _____.

7. A carpenter works with wood; an electrician works with _____.

8. A putty knife is flat; a drill bit is _____.

9. Oil is used to lubricate; varnish is used to _____.

10. Hinges can creak; pipes can _____.

11. A plug has prongs; a hammer has a _____.

12. A Phillips head is a kind of screwdriver; a needle-nose is a kind of
    _____.

13. A rug is used in the living room; linoleum is used in the _____.

14. Stain is used for coloring; bleach is used for _____.

15. Storm windows are used in the winter; screens are used in the
    _____.

Completing Sentence Analogies

Complete the analogies.

1. Burners are part of a stove; blades are part of a _____.

2. Gloves are worn on the hands; goggles are worn on the _____.

3. Walls are made from brick; floors are made from _____.

4. A tape rule is used for measuring; sandpaper is used for _____.

5. An electrician uses a voltage meter; a plumber uses a _____.

6. Black paint is dark; white paint is _____.

7. Wood screws are used in wood; machine screws are used in _____.

8. A saw cuts wood; tin snips cut _____.

9. A paint roller is used on the wall; a paintbrush is used on the _____.

10. A furnace heats; an air conditioner _____.

11. Carpet is on a floor; shingles are on a _____.

12. A sash is part of a window; a step is part of a _____.

13. Screws are put in a hole; lightbulbs are put in a _____.

14. Toggle bolts are used on hollow walls; expansion fasteners are used on _____.

15. Gasoline is made from oil; boards are made from _____.

Modifying Sentence Incongruities

Replace a word or phrase in each sentence that doesn't make sense.

1. Replace the handle if you have a leaky faucet.

2. Rubber cement is used to fill in cracks or spaces between ceramic tiles.

3. A hinge is a type of bolt used on hollow walls.

4. Varnish is a thin layer of superior quality wood glued to an inferior wood.

5. A damper is a movable metal plate that controls the amount of air that goes up the rain spout.

6. An awning is usually made out of aluminum or silicone.

7. Solder is a molten plaster used to join metal parts together.

8. A plane is a type of hammer.

9. Use a hose to raise a car when changing a flat tire.

10. Call an electrician for plumbing problems.

Modifying Sentence Incongruities

Replace a word or phrase in each sentence that doesn't make sense.

1. Rinse the car with alcohol after washing it.

2. A lawn mower has ten wheels.

3. Use a hedge trimmer to cut down a tree.

4. An electric sander is used to smooth concrete.

5. A washer and nut are used with a nail.

6. A ladder can fit inside a toolbox.

7. A sluggish clock can be opened with a chemical drain cleaner.

8. A tool belt is worn around the calf.

9. A wrench is used to drive in nails.

10. There are 5,000 pounds in a ton.

Modifying Sentence Incongruities

Replace a word or phrase in each sentence that doesn't make sense.

1. Construction workers wear slippers on their feet for protection.

2. It is safe to use a ladder on uneven loose gravel.

3. Paint is a coating used to cover Styrofoam surfaces.

4. A wing nut has flared sides you can tighten with your teeth.

5. The place where two pipes meet is called a joist.

6. A circular saw can be used to trim bushes.

7. Grout is used to fill in cracks around rubber tiles.

8. Air conditioners heat the air in the summer.

9. Walls can be made from concrete block, sawdust, or stones.

10. A plumber's snake can be used to open paint cans.

Determining if Statements Are True or False

Write **T** on the line if the statement is true. Write **F** if the statement is false.

_____ 1. A chimney should be professionally inspected five times a year.

_____ 2. Frayed cords on window blinds should be replaced.

_____ 3. Sagging floor beams can be caused by dry rot.

_____ 4. A rafter is a beam found in walls.

_____ 5. A lawn mower is used to cut the grass.

_____ 6. A clogged drain can always be opened by running the water full force.

_____ 7. Spackle is a kind of glue used for mending ceramic.

_____ 8. It is usually best to apply two coats of paint.

_____ 9. Varnish is used for coating and refinishing wood.

_____ 10. If your screen door won't shut, it may be because the springs and door checks are loose.

_____ 11. It's safe to replace an electrical outlet without turning off the electricity.

_____ 12. The best way to check that an outlet is working is to stick a metal object into it.

_____ 13. If there is a strong odor of gas in a room, don't light any matches.

_____ 14. It's a good idea to hammer down and countersink protruding nails.

_____ 15. Broken glass can be mended with glue.

Determining if Statements Are True or False

Write **T** on the line if the statement is true. Write **F** if the statement is false.

_____ 1. A flood always occurs when a sink's washer is worn.

_____ 2. Use powdered graphite to help loosen a sticky lock.

_____ 3. Nothing can be done once a water pipe starts to freeze.

_____ 4. If the burners on a gas range aren't working, check to see if the pilot light is out.

_____ 5. Lawn mower blades should be sharpened periodically.

_____ 6. When the holes in a showerhead close, it's probably because minerals in the water are plugging them.

_____ 7. It won't help keep cold air out if you weather strip windows.

_____ 8. The main switch for a home's electricity is located under the kitchen sink.

_____ 9. Sandpaper can be used for smoothing wood.

_____ 10. Fence posts never need to be replaced.

_____ 11. You should drill a pilot hole for a screw.

_____ 12. Wood screws can be made of solder.

_____ 13. A Phillips head screwdriver has a single-slot head.

_____ 14. Rubbing soap on the threads of a screw makes it easier to turn in the wood.

_____ 15. Sometimes you can use water to clean paintbrushes.

Determining if Statements Are True or False

Write **T** on the line if the statement is true. Write **F** if the statement is false.

_____ 1. When you replace a machine screw, the new one should be exactly the same size as the one you are replacing.

_____ 2. Screws tighten pieces of wood together better than nails.

_____ 3. A round-headed screw will lie flush with the surface.

_____ 4. If a screwdriver slips, it can damage the head of the screw.

_____ 5. You shouldn't start a screw by forcing it into the wood.

_____ 6. Chair legs should be glued instead of joined by screws.

_____ 7. Washable wallpapers can be scrubbed with a coarse brush.

_____ 8. Before washing wallpaper, test a small area that can't easily be seen.

_____ 9. Use a lot of hot, soapy water when washing a painted wall.

_____ 10. Short circuits can cause fires.

_____ 11. Periodically check the cords and plugs of electrical appliances.

_____ 12. Lights that go out in one part of a home and not another indicates a circuit breaker may have tripped.

_____ 13. Turn off the circuit breaker before working on something electrical.

_____ 14. You should always use glue to attach carpets to floors.

_____ 15. You should check the oil in your car every day.

Determining if Statements Are True or False

Write **T** on the line if the statement is true. Write **F** if the statement is false.

_____ 1. Indoor/outdoor carpet is frequently used in bedrooms.

_____ 2. If the electricity goes out, it's a good idea to turn off the lamps and appliances.

_____ 3. Hammers, screwdrivers, and pliers have handles.

_____ 4. Throw out any tool with a dull blade.

_____ 5. All homes are cooled with window unit air conditioners.

_____ 6. A nail can be removed with the claw of a hammer.

_____ 7. Scaffolding is used when preparing a garden.

_____ 8. You should wear goggles or safety glasses when using a chain saw.

_____ 9. A caulking gun is used for hunting animals.

_____ 10. Most stepladders have a fold-down shelf.

_____ 11. A snow shovel and snow blower are useful in cold winter climates.

_____ 12. Metal washers are used to attach drill bits to the drill.

_____ 13. Pipe cutters can be used to tighten screws.

_____ 14. A thermometer measures temperature.

_____ 15. A tape rule can be used for pipe insulation.

Determining if Statements Are True or False

Write **T** on the line if the statement is true. Write **F** if the statement is false.

_____ 1. A level helps determine how straight an object is.

_____ 2. A putty knife is usually used to spread paint.

_____ 3. Metal punches are used for measuring distances.

_____ 4. Pliers are used for grasping, turning, and tightening.

_____ 5. Drill bits attach to the end of a wrench.

_____ 6. Many sizes of screws can be bought in a hardware store.

_____ 7. A monkey wrench can be adjusted to different sizes.

_____ 8. Roof shingles are frequently made out of rubber.

_____ 9. A C-clamp can hold pieces of wood together.

_____ 10. Plaster is frequently used to cover bookshelves.

_____ 11. Epoxy and rubber cement are types of floor coverings.

_____ 12. Extra nails and screws can be stored in boxes or jars.

_____ 13. A patio can be made from brick, flagstone, and barrels.

_____ 14. It is a good idea to have extra lightbulbs.

_____ 15. Many newer toilets are designed to conserve water.

Comparing Sentence Content

Write **S** on the line if the sentences mean about the same. Write **D** if the sentences have different meanings.

_____ 1. Strike the nail with a hammer.
Hit the nail with a hammer.

_____ 2. Handling any electrical appliance requires care.
Use care when working with electrical appliances.

_____ 3. Your garbage disposal is made to grind soft foods.
Don't grind metals, glass, or plastics in your garbage disposal.

_____ 4. Use rubber or contact cement to glue the dish pieces back together.
Seal the edges of the plate with an adhesive.

_____ 5. Constant banging and slamming is hard on a door.
A door should never be slammed.

_____ 6. A sagging floor is dangerous and should be repaired.
Guard against the dangers of a sagging floor by fixing the problem.

_____ 7. Dampness in a house always comes from moisture on the pipes.
There are many causes for excess moisture in a home.

_____ 8. Turn a screw to the right when tightening it.
When tightening a screw, turn it clockwise.

_____ 9. Water vapor from the bathroom can cause wall damage.
Excessive moisture from various sources affects walls in rooms.

_____ 10. Mend the rip with a matching piece of plastic.
Patch the tear with a piece of the same plastic material.

Comparing Sentence Content

Write **S** on the line if the sentences mean about the same. Write **D** if the sentences have different meanings.

_____ 1. Spread the prongs with your fingers.
Use your fingers to spread the prongs.

_____ 2. Trim away the excess tape.
Don't let any of the cloth extend over the edges.

_____ 3. Varnishing can be tricky, tacky work.
Varnish, although sticky, helps seal the wood.

_____ 4. Screen blocks admit light and air.
Light and air can come through screen blocks.

_____ 5. It is best to call a professional to make your furnace repairs.
Tackling heating problems can be a real challenge.

_____ 6. To insure that wood won't move when cutting, put it in a vise.
A vise will hold wood steady when you are cutting it.

_____ 7. Leaky faucets are a nuisance.
Home repairs should be completed quickly.

_____ 8. Stain darkens wood.
Darken wood with stain.

_____ 9. Gutters should be cleaned of debris.
Debris should be cleaned from gutters.

_____ 10. Sandpaper will smooth rough edges.
Rough edges can give you splinters.

Comparing Sentence Content

Write **S** on the line if the sentences mean about the same. Write **D** if the sentences have different meanings.

_____ 1. Dig a hole, keeping the sides straight.
Keep the sides vertical when digging a hole.

_____ 2. A wheelbarrow is used for lawn work.
Many electrical appliances help keep a lawn beautiful.

_____ 3. Walls lower than three feet will probably not require a permit.
A permit is needed when building an addition on your home.

_____ 4. Dry ingredients are mixed before water is added.
Mix the dry ingredients before adding water.

_____ 5. A retaining wall is built with concrete block.
Concrete block is used to build a retaining wall.

_____ 6. A drain clog can be loosened with a plunger.
Call a plumber if you have a drain problem.

_____ 7. Check the circuit breaker if the lights go out.
If all the appliances stop working, there must be a storm.

_____ 8. Mortar sticks masonry units together.
Masonry units are joined with mortar.

_____ 9. Slate can range widely in color.
Slate is frequently used in patios.

_____ 10. Use a saw to cut wood.
When cutting wood, use a saw.

Evaluating Information

Write **Yes** on the blank if it is something you would do when you **paint**. Write **No** if it is not something you would do.

_____ 1. Cover the old paint with one thick coat of new paint.

_____ 2. Apply two coats of paint.

_____ 3. Look at the paint samples in daylight and under electric light before making a final decision.

_____ 4. Use high-gloss paint on your ceiling because it is so shiny.

_____ 5. Wash latex-painted walls with oil and epoxy.

_____ 6. Clean up paint drippings right away.

_____ 7. Remove hardware and cover plates before painting.

_____ 8. Use a paint roller or wide brush on the woodwork and trim.

_____ 9. Select a brush that best suits the job.

_____ 10. Paint large, flat areas with a narrow brush.

_____ 11. Cover the furniture and floor with a drop cloth.

_____ 12. Wash the walls before painting.

_____ 13. Put lots of paint on the brush or roller.

_____ 14. Apply a coat of primer before using latex paint over oil-based paint.

_____ 15. Paint the ceiling black if the walls are white.

Evaluating Information

Write **Yes** on the blank if it is something you would do if a **sink drain is clogged**. Write **No** if it is not something you would do.

_____ 1. Push a broom handle down the pipe to loosen the obstruction.

_____ 2. Use a plunger to loosen the obstruction.

_____ 3. Run the water hard to push the clog down the drain.

_____ 4. Take all the pipes apart and find the clog.

_____ 5. Use a chemical drain cleaner to loosen the clog.

_____ 6. Let the clog sit for a couple of days because time will work the clog loose.

_____ 7. Use a plumber's snake to clear the drain.

_____ 8. Once the clog is cleared, run the water for a few minutes.

_____ 9. Buy a new sink.

_____ 10. Ignore it.

_____ 11. Try plunging it. If that doesn't work, use a chemical cleaner.

_____ 12. Remove all the water and debris from the basin.

_____ 13. Permanently turn off all the water to all pipes in the house.

_____ 14. Turn the faucet on and let it run for 20 minutes.

_____ 15. Call a plumber if all of your efforts fail.

Evaluating Information

Write **Yes** on the blank if it is something you would do when your **window air conditioner won't start**. Write **No** if it is not something you would do.

_____ 1. Check the circuit breaker to see if it has tripped.

_____ 2. Spread the plug prongs out so they fit firmly into the outlet.

_____ 3. Jiggle something in the outlet to see if it's working.

_____ 4. Replace the filter, plug, and outer covering.

_____ 5. Make sure the unit is plugged in properly.

_____ 6. Check the outside temperature to see if it is still hot out.

_____ 7. Set the dials properly.

_____ 8. Take off the cover and vacuum out the dust inside the unit.

_____ 9. Check for a faulty plug.

_____ 10. Throw it out and then go buy a new air conditioner.

_____ 11. Ask your neighbor if his air conditioner works.

_____ 12. Clean the filter, adjust the dials, and check the plug.

_____ 13. Wait until next summer to see if it works then.

_____ 14. Call a repairman if none of your actions work.

_____ 15. Take it apart and see if you can fix it.

Evaluating Information

Write **Yes** on the blank if it is something you would do to **use a ladder safely**.
Write **No** if it is not something you would do.

_____ 1. Use a homemade ladder made of balsam wood.

_____ 2. Use a ladder horizontally without supports.

_____ 3. Place a ladder on firm, level ground.

_____ 4. Make sure your feet and the rungs are free from grease.

_____ 5. Sufficiently overlap the sections of an extension ladder so it's sturdy.

_____ 6. Face the ladder, hold it with both hands, and place your feet firmly on each rung as you climb.

_____ 7. Carry large, heavy items up and down the ladder.

_____ 8. Anchor the ladder with a rope.

_____ 9. Hold the ladder with one hand as you climb up and down.

_____ 10. Use an aluminum ladder to do electrical work.

_____ 11. Replace any rotted steps on a wooden ladder.

_____ 12. Ignore the rotted steps.

_____ 13. Link several ladders together to get up high.

_____ 14. Only have one person on the ladder at a time.

_____ 15. Add a few steps if it's too short.

Evaluating Information

Write **Yes** on the blank if it is something you would do if your **vacuum isn't working properly**. Write **No** if it is not something you would do.

_____ 1. Check the condition of the bristles on the roller.

_____ 2. Throw it out.

_____ 3. Replace the cord if it's worn or frayed.

_____ 4. Check to see if something is lodged in the hose.

_____ 5. Stick it in the closet and ignore the whole thing.

_____ 6. Check the plug and outlet.

_____ 7. Change the bag if it's full.

_____ 8. Hire a cleaning service to do the vacuuming from now on.

_____ 9. Bang the vacuum on the floor in case something is stuck.

_____ 10. Make sure the on/off switch is working.

_____ 11. Wash off the roller, the inner canister, and motor.

_____ 12. Plug the vacuum in, turn it on, and take the motor apart.

_____ 13. Check that all the dials are set correctly.

_____ 14. Replace all the hoses, belts, and wheels.

_____ 15. Take it to a repair shop if you can't fix it.

Using Deductive Reasoning

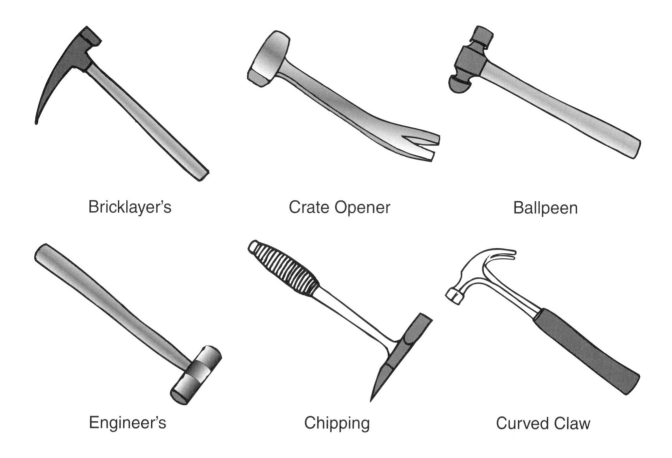

Bricklayer's   Crate Opener   Ballpeen

Engineer's   Chipping   Curved Claw

Use the clues to determine which hammer the carpenter used. Cross off hammers until you are left with one. The hammer that is left is the one the carpenter used.

1. The hammer was not pointed.

2. It did not have the title of a professional in its name.

3. It was not rounded on one end.

4. It was not used for prying off the lids of wooden crates.

5. He not only needed the hammer for driving in nails but also for removing nails.

Which hammer did he use? _____

Using Deductive Reasoning

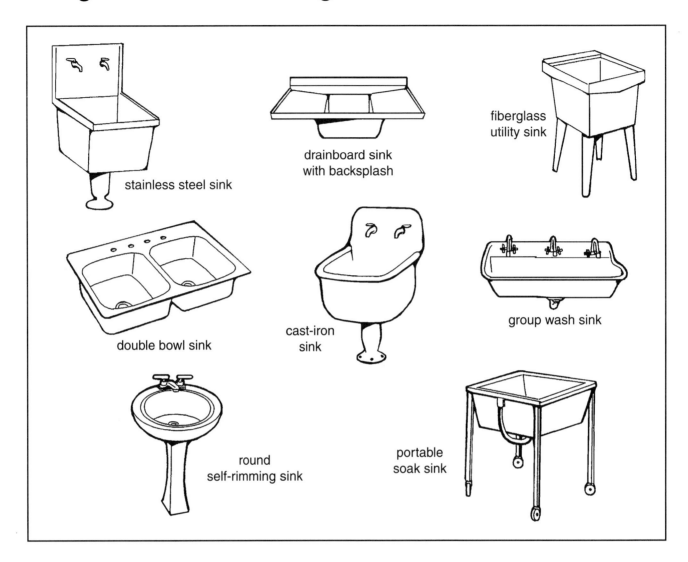

Use the clues to determine which sink the Smiths bought for their home. Cross off sinks until you are left with one. The one that is left is the sink the Smiths bought.

1. They didn't want a cast iron or fiberglass sink.

2. The group wash sink was unnecessary.

3. The portable sink was too expensive.

4. A double bowl sink or one with a drainboard was too large for the area.

5. Ms. Smith wanted a sink with only one faucet.

Which sink did they buy? _____

Using Deductive Reasoning

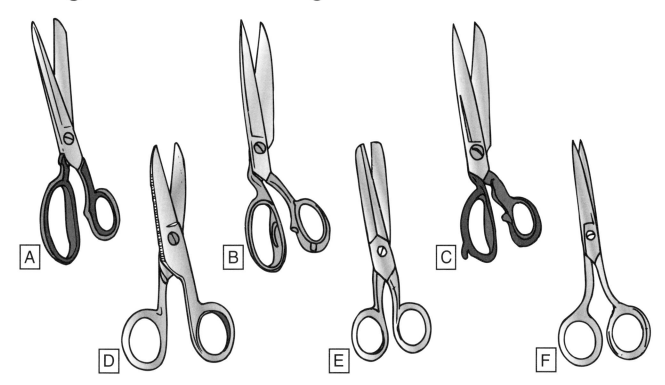

- A Straight-handle standard duty shears
- B Bent-handle standard duty shears
- C Bent-handle extra heavy-duty shears
- D Electrician's scissors
- E Blunt-point pocket scissors
- F Double sharp point scissors

Use the clues to determine which pair of shears or scissors the tailor used. Cross off pairs until you are left with one. The pair that is left is the one the tailor used.

1. He needed ones with a sharp tip, so the blunt-point ones were eliminated.

2. Because he was cutting material, he didn't need extra heavy-duty shears.

3. Since he was not cutting wires, he didn't need the electrician's scissors.

4. He was afraid he would make a mistake if he used double sharp scissors.

5. Out of the two remaining shears, he decided to use the ones that were not straight handled so the material wasn't lifted too high while he was cutting.

Which pair of scissors or shears did he use? _____

Using Deductive Reasoning

	Supervisor	Basement	Porch	Attic
Rex				
Chris				
Skip				
Bob				

Four carpenters (Rex, Chris, Skip, Bob) are doing work at a house. One of them is the supervisor. The other three are working in three different areas: the basement, the porch, and the attic.

Use the clues to determine who is the supervisor and where each carpenter is working.

1. From where he is working, Rex can hear the carpenter who is working on the porch.

2. Skip is not working in the basement.

3. From his location, Bob can see the supervisor.

4. Skip is using his skills to repair the beams in the attic.

5. Rex and the supervisor discussed the shelving Rex will build in the basement.

Using Deductive Reasoning

	Plumber	Mason	Roofer	Painter
Pete				
Paul				
Pat				
Preston				

Pete, Paul, Pat, and Preston are all contractors. They are a plumber, mason, roofer, and painter.

Use the clues to determine each one's profession.

1. Pete, who is not the painter, drives to work with the mason.

2. The painter bowls with Pat on Tuesdays and goes to Rotary Club meetings with Preston.

3. Preston is not the roofer.

4. The mason and the painter are the only two who attend Rotary Club meetings.

5. Pete is afraid of heights, so he isn't the roofer.

****

Jack, Alice, Candie, and Tony are two sets of workers. Tony does plumbing but not with Jack. Candie does landscaping but not with Alice.

Which pair does the plumbing? _____

Which pair does the landscaping? _____

Picture/Paragraph Comprehension

People who experience some form of brain dysfunction often have difficulty with visual skills. They may have trouble interpreting what they see. They may have difficulty ascertaining specific items in a picture from the picture as a whole. They may have visual-spatial difficulties and be unable to determine where the items in a picture are in relation to the other items. Thus, this section presents several pictures with questions that target those difficulties to provide a structured approach for assisting in remediation of those skill areas.

Frequently, your client may be able to comprehend, manipulate, and deduce answers for stimuli that involves only a few words or a sentence, but his skills deteriorate as the length is increased to the paragraph level. This section includes paragraph comprehension tasks in order to help your client improve his ability to comprehend and retain lengthier written information.

The tasks in this section provide pictures related to painting and home repairs. The paragraphs relate to home repair situations your client may have or may encounter.

Answering Questions About a Picture

Look at the picture and answer the questions.

1. What is going to happen? _____

2. Which room is being painted? _____

3. What painting equipment is in the room? _____

4. What is near the stepladder? _____

5. What is in the paint tray? _____

6. What color is the paint? _____

7. Is the window open or closed? _____

8. Is the floor covered? _____

9. What furniture is in the room? _____

10. Are there curtains on the window? _____

Answering Questions About a Picture

Look at the picture and answer the questions.

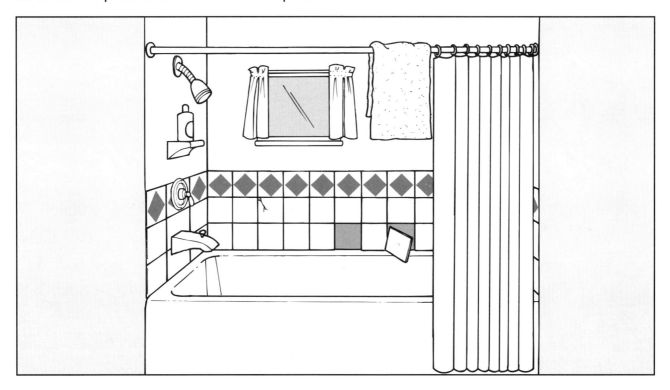

1. What room is in the picture? _____

2. What needs to be fixed? _____

3. How many tiles are missing? _____

4. What design is on one row of the tiles? _____

5. Is there a window in the bathroom? _____

6. Are there curtains on the window? _____

7. Does the bathroom have a shower? _____

8. What is hanging over the curtain rod? _____

9. Is the towel striped or plain? _____

10. What is on the shower wall? _____

Answering Questions About a Picture

Look at the picture and answer the questions.

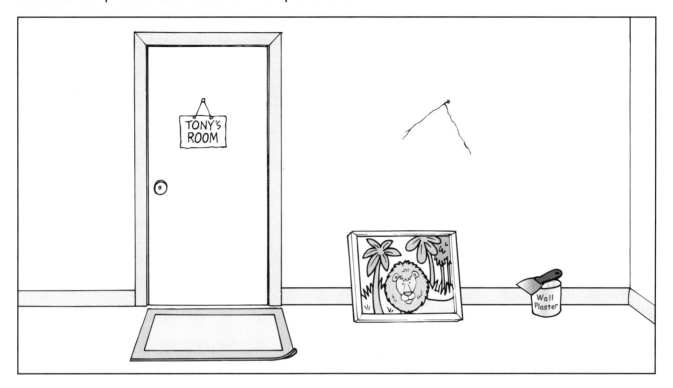

1. What needs to be fixed? _____

2. How many cracks are in the wall? _____

3. What is stuck in the wall near the cracks? _____

4. Is the door open or closed? _____

5. Where is the can of plaster? _____

6. What is on top of the can of plaster? _____

7. What is in the picture that is to be hung? _____

8. Where is the picture? _____

9. Whose room is it? _____

10. What is on the floor in front of the door? _____

Answering Questions About a Picture

Look at the picture and answer the questions.

1. What is at the top of the railings?

2. How many steps are there?

3. How many steps need to be fixed?

4. How many windows can you see?

5. What is below the window on the right?

6. Where is the wood to fix the step?

7. What is lying on the wood?

8. Has the wood been cut for the step?

9. What kind of saw is being used?

10. Where are the nails and hammer?

Answering Questions About a Picture

Look at the picture and answer the questions.

1. Is the house one or two stories? _____

2. What needs to be fixed? _____

3. Where are the new shingles? _____

4. What tools and supplies are near the shingles? _____

5. How many windows are on the front of the house? _____

6. What is below the window on the left? _____

7. Which window has shutters? _____

8. Who is coming out of the house? _____

9. Is the door open or closed? _____

10. Where is the ladder? _____

Comprehending Information in a Paragraph

Read the paragraph and answer the questions.

Replacing a Wooden Step

To replace a step, first buy a new piece of wood. Before you nail the piece down, paint the underside of it with wood preservative. You can buy wood preservative at a hardware or home improvement store. Use the preservative on the stringer supports too. Next, nail the new board in place. Countersink the nails with a tool called a nail set. Then, fill the holes over the nail heads with plastic wood or some other kind of wood filler. Finally, paint or stain the step to match the rest of the steps.

1. What two things should be painted with wood preservative?

2. Where can you buy wood preservative?

3. What do you do after you use the wood preservative?

4. What do you use to countersink a nail?

5. What do you use to fill the holes over the nail heads?

6. What can you use so the new step matches the other steps?

7. If you don't know what a stringer support is, where could you find out about it?

8. What else do you know about this topic?

Comprehending Information in a Paragraph

Read the paragraph and answer the questions.

Sweating Pipes

Cold water pipes can be found in the basement ceiling or leading into the bathroom or kitchen sink. If the pipes are exposed, they collect moisture from the air, or sweat. Pipes sweat more often in the winter when the house is heated. The moisture, or condensation, drips onto the floor and can cause damage. An easy way to solve the problem is to wrap the pipes with insulating material. Fiberglass insulation is an ideal material found in any hardware or building supply store. Purchase insulation that is waterproof or has a waterproof outside covering. If you use waterproof insulation, you only need to wrap the pipe once. If you use a non-waterproof insulation, you will need to add a waterproof wrapping over the insulation.

1. What can happen to cold water pipes if exposed?

2. What is the moisture on pipes called?

3. What kind of wrapping material will prevent condensation?

4. Where can you buy it?

5. What kind of fiberglass wrapping material should you get?

6. If you use waterproof insulation, how many times do you need to wrap the pipe?

7. What should you do if you buy non-waterproof insulation?

8. What else do you know about this topic?

Comprehending Information in a Paragraph

Read the paragraph and answer the questions.

Creaking Stairs

It's easy to reduce or eliminate the creaking in stairs that are open. Here are three suggestions.

- For a temporary solution, spray a silicone lubricant into the creaking area. This area will frequently be where the risers meet the tread.
- Insert a small wooden wedge between the tread and the stringer.
- Insert screws up through the treads into the risers.

If your staircase is enclosed, drive finishing nails along the tread into the stringer on the top of the stair. You can also use a silicone lubricating spray to eliminate the creak.

1. How many ways can you fix a creak in stairs that are open?

2. How many ways can you fix a creak in stairs that are enclosed?

3. What kind of spray can eliminate a creak?

4. Where are creaks frequently found?

5. Where can you insert a wedge to stop a creak?

6. What can you put through the treads and into the risers on an open staircase?

7. What kind of nails can you use on the surface of a step?

8. Where would you put these nails?

9. What else do you know about this topic?

Resources

Evidence-Based Research Articles Regarding Therapy for Cognitive-Communication Disorders

American Speech-Language-Hearing Association. (2006). *Treatment efficacy summary: Aphasia resulting from left hemisphere stroke.* Retrieved 12/23/06 from www.asha.org.

American Speech-Language-Hearing Association. (2006). *Treatment efficacy summary: Cognitive-communication disorders resulting from right hemisphere brain damage.* Retrieved 12/23/06 from www.asha.org.

American Speech-Language-Hearing Association. (2006). *Treatment efficacy summary: Cognitive-communication disorders resulting from traumatic brain injury.* Retrieved 12/23/06 from www.asha.org.

Boghal, S.K., Teasell, R.W., Foley, N.C., & Speechley, M.R. (2003). Rehabilitation of aphasia: More is better. *Topics in Stroke Rehabilitation, 10(2)*, 66-76.

Carney, N., Chestnut, R., Maynard, H., Mann, N.C., Patterson, P., & Helfand, M. (1999). Effect of cognitive rehabilitation on outcomes for persons with traumatic brain injury: A systematic review. *Journal of Head Trauma Research, 14(3)*, 277-307.

Cicerone, K.D., Dahlberg, C., Kalmar, K., Langenbahn, D.M., Malec, J.F., Bergquist, T.F., et al. (2000). Evidence-based cognitive rehabilitation: Recommendations for clinical practice. *Archives of Physical Medicine and Rehabilitation, 81(12)*, 1596-1615.

Cicerone, K.D., Dahlberg, C., Malec, J., Langenbahn, D.M., Felicetti, T., Kneipp, S., et al. (2005). Evidence-based cognitive rehabilitation: Updated review of the literature from 1998 through 2002. *Archives of Physical Medicine and Rehabilitation, 86(8)*, 1681-1692.

Coelho, C.A., DeRuyter, F., & Stein, M. (1996). Treatment efficacy: Cognitive-communication disorders resulting from traumatic brain injury in adults. *Journal of Speech and Hearing Research, 39(5)*, S5-S17.

Winocur, G., Craik, F.I.M., Levine, B., Robertson, I.H., Binns, M.A., Alexander, M., et al. (2007). Cognitive rehabilitation in the elderly: Overview and future directions. *Journal of the International Neuropsychological Society, 13*, 166-171.

Books on Cognitive Communication

Elman, R. (Ed.). (2006). *Group treatment of neurogenic communication disorders: The expert clinician's approach.* (2nd ed.). San Diego: Plural Publishing, Inc.

Helms-Estabrooks, N., & Albert, M.L. (2005). *Manual of aphasia and aphasia therapy.* Austin, TX: Pro-Ed, Inc.

Hillis, A. (2002). *The handbook of adult language disorders.* NY: Psychology Press, an imprint of the Taylor & Francis Group.

Keith, R.L., & Schumacher, J.G. (2001). *Speech and language rehabilitation.* (4th ed.). Austin, TX: Pro-Ed, Inc.

LaPointe, L.L. (2005). *Aphasia and related neurogenic language disorders.* (3rd ed.). NYC: Thieme Publishers.

Sarno, M.T., & Peters, J.F. (Eds). (2004). *The aphasia handbook: A guide for stroke and brain injury survivors and their families.* NYC: National Aphasia Association.

Books on Home Repair/Home Maintenance

Black & Decker. (2001). *The complete photo guide to home improvement: Over 1700 photos, 250 step-by-step projects.* Chanhassen, MN: Creative Publishing International.

Creative Publishing International. (2004). *The complete photo guide to home repair: With 350 projects and 2300 photos.* Chanhassen, MN: Author.

Family Handyman Magazine Editors. (2005). *Complete do-it-yourself manual: Completely revised and updated.* Pleasantville, NY: Reader's Digest.

Reader's Digest Editors. (1996). *New fix-it-yourself manual: How to repair, clean, and maintain anything and everything in and around your home.* Pleasantville, NY: Reader's Digest.

Sussman, J., & Glakas-Tenet, S. (2002). *Dare to repair: A do-it-herself guide to fixing (almost) anything around the house.* NYC: HarperCollins Publishers.

Organizations

American Speech-Language-Hearing Association (ASHA)
Promotes the interests of and provides the highest quality services for professionals in audiology, speech-language pathology, and speech and hearing science; advocates for people with communication disabilities

www.asha.org
800-498-2071 (members)
800-638-8255 (non-members)

Aphasia Hope Foundation
Promotes research into the prevention and cure of aphasia as well as ensuring that all survivors of aphasia and their caregivers are aware of and have access to the best possible treatments available; the largest collaborative online resource for aphasia

www.aphasiahope.org
866-449-5804 (toll free)

Brain Injury Association of America (BIA)
Provides information, education, and support to persons currently living with TBI, their families, and professionals working with individuals who have sustained a TBI

www.biausa.org
800-444-6443

National Aphasia Association (NAA)
Promotes public education, research, rehabilitation, and support services to assist people with aphasia and their families

www.aphasia.org
800-922-4622

National Institute of Neurological Disorders & Stroke (NINDS)
Supports and conducts research on the brain and nervous system; fosters the training of investigators in the basic and clinical neurosciences; and seeks better understanding, diagnosis, treatment, and prevention of neurological disorders

www.ninds.nih.gov
800-352-9424

National Rehabilitation Information Center (NARIC)
Provides information to the disability and rehabilitation community through online publications, searchable databases, and timely reference and referral data

www.naric.com
800-346-2742

National Stroke Association (NSA)
Provides information and resources for stroke survivors, their families, and caregivers

www.stroke.org
800-787-6537 (STROKES)

References

Liles, M.D., & Liles, R.M. (1974). *Good housekeeping guide to fixing things around the house.*
    NY: Good Housekeeping Books.

Answer Key

The most likely answers are listed here. Accept other logical, appropriate answers as correct.

HOME ACTIVITIES

page 9
bureau/dresser, sofa/couch, rocking chair, piano, desk, picture, lamp, table, alarm clock

page 10
ladle, oven mitt, bowl, rolling pin, cutting board, baking pan, pitcher, mug, scissors

page 11
corn, grapes, bananas, cheese, strawberries, turkey, cabbage/lettuce, cake, pepper

page 12

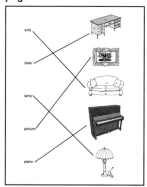

page 13

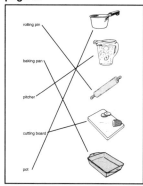

page 14

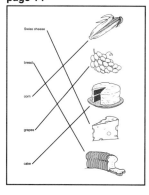

page 15
coffeepot
cardboard box
rocking chair
washing machine
birdbath
windowsill
picture frame
bookshelf
bathtub
sweatshirt
paperweight
end table
milk carton
cookie sheet
can opener

page 16
cheese shredder
butcher knife
soup spoon
aluminum foil
pillowcase
shower curtain
frying pan
picnic table
cookie jar
suitcase
salt shaker
coffee mug
hand mixer
mixing bowl
lightbulb

page 17
microwave oven
hairspray
nail file
vacuum cleaner
potato peeler
shaving cream
remote control
bath towel
gas stove
hand lotion
dustpan
medicine cabinet
soap dish
light switch
water faucet

page 18
1. f   4. a   7. g   10. c
2. h   5. j   8. d
3. e   6. b   9. i

page 19
1. i   4. h   7. b   10. f
2. e   5. d   8. a
3. g   6. j   9. c

page 20
1. i   4. b   7. h   10. g
2. c   5. e   8. d
3. j   6. f   9. a

page 21
1. evergreen, pine
2. knife
3. phone
4. necklace
5. money
6. car, truck
7. hanger
8. cart, basket
9. needle and thread
10. cough medicine, cold medicine, aspirin
11. towel
12. comb, brush
13. watering can
14. bureau/dresser, desk
15. bedroom

page 22
1. sidewalk
2. cookbook
3. spatula, flipper
4. ketchup, mustard
5. department store
6. picture, tapestry
7. piano
8. purse, backpack
9. toothbrush
10. oven
11. pillow
12. mixer
13. washer
14. breakfast
15. pen, pencil

page 23
1. television
2. hose, sprinkler
3. mirror
4. fan, air conditioner
5. coat, sweater
6. bucket
7. salt, pepper
8. paper
9. sofa/couch
10. cookie sheet
11. shovel
12. closet
13. garden
14. canisters
15. staple, paper clip

page 24
1. door, toaster
2. book
3. tree, table
4. closet, book
5. pants, jacket
6. stove
7. apple
8. shirt
9. flower
10. glasses
11. sink
12. car, bicycle
13. bed
14. gloves, clock
15. coat, fish
16. suitcase

17. lamp, hair dryer
18. knife, ice skates, chain saw
19. dresser, desk
20. candle
21. table, chair
22. pencil
23. pen
24. picture
25. hat
26. brush
27. shirt, coat
28. belt
29. lamp
30. sofa, chair

page 25
1. jar, pot
2. flashlight
3. chair, jacket, shirt
4. jacket, pants
5. watering can, pitcher
6. room, house
7. lamp, window
8. TV, computer, door
9. shoes
10. chair
11. pants
12. purse, backpack
13. light
14. needle, face
15. flower
16. fingers, hammer
17. windows
18. tree, car
19. freezer, cupboard
20. door
21. hose
22. envelope
23. meat, dog
24. rug, scarf
25. bed
26. sieve, colander
27. dog, cat
28. tree
29. roof, car
30. peach, cherry

page 26
1. yardstick
2. feather
3. teenager
4. cola
5. rope
6. cookie
7. house
8. iron
9. ocean
10. scream
11. snow
12. frying pan
13. attack dog
14. kitten
15. morning

page 27
1. toothpick
2. sofa
3. infant
4. lamp

5. potato chip
6. dill pickle
7. second
8. ice
9. cracker
10. whispering
11. licorice
12. dough
13. jet plane
14. lime
15. steak knife

page 28
Laundry: washer, dryer, detergent, basket
Bills: the bills, checks, envelopes, stamps
Pet care: food, water, toys, vet
Plant: soil, plant, pot, water

page 29
Meal: food, plates, dishes, glasses
Hair: comb, brush, shampoo, mirror, hairspray
Photo album: photos, album, labels, pen
Kitchen: bucket, rag, detergent, mop

page 31
Spices
1. dill
2. cloves
3. ginger
4. thyme
5. basil
6. garlic
7. salt
8. nutmeg
9. pepper
10. sage

Clothing
1. shirt
2. pants
3. scarf
4. socks
5. shoes
6. slip
7. gloves
8. coat
9. belt
10. skirt

page 32
Things in a Kitchen
1. pans
2. fork
3. bowl
4. cups
5. jars
6. sink
7. towel
8. table
9. spoon
10. stove

Things in a Bathroom
1. towel
2. soap
3. tub
4. curtain
5. mirror
6. scale
7. hamper

8. tissues
9. sink
10. razor

page 33
Things in a Living Room
1. sofa
2. carpet
3. clock
4. lamp
5. plants
6. curtain
7. books
8. chair
9. closet
10. end table

Cooking Words
1. bake
2. boil
3. broil
4. brown
5. roast
6. simmer
7. warm
8. steam
9. heat
10. toast

page 34
1. She put roses in the vase.
2. Preheat the oven to 350°.
3. He sewed the button on his shirt.
4. What are we having for dinner?
5. The timer on the oven went off.
6. We went to Chicago for our vacation.
7. After the kids left for school, she went to the store.
8. He vacuums downstairs on Friday mornings.
9. The vacuum needed a new bag.
10. He told his son to clean his bedroom.

page 35
1. When do you think you will be finished with your chores?
2. Please lock the door on your way out.
3. They planted vegetables in their garden.
4. The stuffed turkey roasted for five hours.
5. Leona always dusts before she vacuums.
6. There was no more room in the closet.
7. There wasn't enough milk for everyone.
8. Our mail gets delivered after 3:00.
9. The plants started drooping because they needed water.
10. The cleaning supplies were under the sink.

page 36
1. When the electricity went out, they lit some candles.

2. Jeff made an apple pie for dessert.
3. Coupons save you money when buying food.
4. There was a box of tissues on the counter.
5. There was too much salt in the soup.
6. They prepared dinner for their relatives.
7. What are we having for dessert?
8. What color should we paint the bedroom?
9. Would you please wash the windows?
10. Put the groceries on the kitchen table.

page 37
storm, two, louder, lightning, suddenly, house, oil, living, flashlight, drawer, glad

page 38
go, newspaper, mornings, sale, home, old, bidders, own, knew, gift, happy

page 39
income, time, several, kitchen, oven, food, bills, days, portion, money, savings

page 40
Andrew, vacation, ocean, suitcases, cat, through, windows, newspaper, ready, car, sunny

page 41
Set A: 3, 5, 1, 4, 2
getting ready in the morning
Set B: 4, 1, 5, 3, 2
changing the sheets/making the bed
Set C: 2, 4, 5, 3, 1
having a cup of coffee
Set D: 1, 4, 3, 5, 2
planting a garden

page 42
Set A: 6, 2, 5, 3, 1, 4
grilling hamburgers
Set B: 2, 1, 4, 6, 3, 5
washing windows
Set C: 1, 6, 5, 4, 3, 2
doing laundry
Set D: 3, 4, 1, 5, 6, 2
emptying the trash/taking out the garbage

page 43
Set A: 4, 7, 6, 2, 3, 1, 5
taking a bath/shower
Set B: 3, 7, 1, 5, 4, 2, 6
writing a letter
Set C: 5, 2, 6, 1, 7, 4, 3
going somewhere in the car/driving a car

page 44
6:00 got up
6:30 ate breakfast
7:00 raked leaves
8:30 visited Rebecca

9:30 Dawn's house
12:00 lunch
1:00 went swimming
3:00 went home
4:30 watching a movie

page 45
9:00 business meeting
11:00 dance class
12:00 lunch
1:00 shopping
3:00 drove home
3:30 watching a movie
4:00 asleep

pages 47-49
Answers will vary.

page 50
TV: cord, channels, programs, news, movie
Plant: water, plant food, dirt, sunlight, pot
Mail: letters, envelopes, bills, delivered, stamps
Suitcase: pack, clothing, handle, trip, carry
Home: residence, roof, yard, rooms, basement
Lamp: shade, light, bulb, cord, switch

page 51
Cereal: breakfast, bowl, milk, crispy, eat
Chair: furniture, legs, sit, seat, back
Refrigerator: shelves, door, cold, freezer, crisper
Music: harmony, melody, notes, singer, radio
Shoes: heel, shoe, laces, feet, leather
Stove: pan, burner, cook, heat, dial

page 52
Kitchen: plates, glasses, bowls, milk, food, measuring cups, coffee cup, dishes
Wash clothes: washer, water, basket, dryer, dirty clothes, detergent, fabric softener
Salad: lettuce, tomatoes, onion, cucumber, radish, celery
Sewing: cloth, thread, pins, needle, scissors, tape measure, mend, thimble, patterns
Money: quarter, nickel, dollar, dime, half dollar, penny

page 53
Pets: canary, hamster, dog, parrot, horse, cat
Weather: snow, hail, sleet, rain, clear, sunny, windy
Toys: ball, truck, doll, blocks, teddy bear, puzzles
Plants: vine, glass, tree, flower, fern, cactus, bush, shrub
Bedroom: pillow, mirror, blanket, bed, alarm clock, bureau, dresser

page 54
1. spices
2. measurements
3. rooms in a home
4. meat
5. things in a bathroom
6. place setting
7. chores
8. eggs
9. furniture
10. vegetables
11. trees
12. things on a bed
13. fruit
14. dairy products
15. window coverings

page 55
1. things to drink out of
2. pies
3. nuts
4. breads
5. hair color
6. fish
7. drinks, beverages
8. containers
9. flooring
10. bed sizes
11. kitchen appliances
12. clothing
13. light sources
14. flowers
15. shellfish, seafood

page 56
1. pets
2. footwear
3. things to sit on
4. poultry, birds
5. things to read
6. money
7. cheese
8. potatoes
9. things that cut
10. cakes
11. things related to a birthday
12. things used with hair
13. parts of a plant/flower
14. picnic food
15. fabric, material

page 58
1. vacuum cleaner
2. watch
3. sugar
4. lamp
5. couch, sofa
6. mirror
7. carpet, rug
8. microwave oven
9. knife
10. towel
11. hanger
12. picture
13. sink
14. table
15. coffee

page 59
1. shoe
2. spoon
3. soap
4. book
5. egg
6. shirt
7. toothbrush
8. TV
9. garden
10. needle, sewing machine
11. car
12. chair
13. aspirin
14. gloves, mittens
15. pen

page 60
1. pants
2. thermometer
3. eyeglasses
4. pillow
5. ketchup
6. hose
7. corn
8. phone
9. ice cubes
10. flower
11. pencil
12. curtain
13. ring
14. bed
15. spaghetti

page 61
1. cars
2. noodles
3. sweater
4. fork
5. carpeting
6. pudding
7. workbench
8. sun
9. newspaper
10. plate
11. swimming
12. cans
13. tack
14. glove
15. flounder

page 62
1. dish towel
2. tuna
3. sink
4. milk
5. brush
6. carpet
7. socks
8. dishes
9. curtains
10. tree
11. zippers
12. toast
13. alley
14. drapes
15. slicer

page 63
bird, mitten, eggs, bed

page 64
plane, house, oven, radio

page 65
1. floor
2. door
3. pepper
4. cake
5. cookbook
6. watching
7. sofa, couch
8. salad
9. brushed
10. vegetable
11. lamp
12. beans, corn
13. clothes
14. vacuumed
15. sweet

page 66
1. hot tea, coffee
2. plate
3. bedroom
4. sour
5. bed
6. meat
7. flashlight
8. paper
9. knife
10. oven
11. hot
12. green beans, peas
13. washing
14. washing
15. potato salad

page 67
1. ice cream/cans, cupboard/freezer
2. dinner/breakfast, morning/evening
3. lumber/groceries, grocery store/lumberyard
4. morning/afternoon
5. plumbing/towing, car broke down/sink began to leak
6. drawers/windows
7. salt/sugar
8. empty/full
9. zipper/drawer, dresser/dress
10. band/battery

page 68
1. milk/sugar, canister on the counter/in the refrigerator
2. a maple tree/flowers, flower box/yard
3. bulb/cord
4. nail polish/furniture polish, nail polish/rag
5. kitchen sink/bathroom closet
6. washcloths/sheets
7. pictures/windows
8. ten minutes/45 minutes
9. on/off
10. hamburgers/cake, dessert/dinner

page 69
1. winter/spring
2. pickle/yellow
3. living room/garden
4. rake/spatula, flip the pancakes/gather the leaves into a pile
5. cups/teaspoons, on his cereal/in the cookie batter
6. broom/paper towels, washed the windows/swept the floor
7. strainer/pot
8. 650°/375°
9. library/drugstore, buy aspirin/get some books
10. sugar/salt

page 70

1. F	5. F	9. F	13. F
2. T	6. T	10. F	14. T
3. T	7. T	11. F	15. F
4. F	8. T	12. T	

page 71

1. T	5. F	9. F	13. F
2. T	6. T	10. T	14. T
3. F	7. F	11. T	15. T
4. T	8. T	12. T	

page 72

1. F	5. T	9. F	13. T
2. T	6. T	10. T	14. F
3. T	7. F	11. F	15. T
4. F	8. T	12. F	

page 73

1. T	5. F	9. T	13. T
2. F	6. F	10. F	14. F
3. T	7. T	11. T	15. F
4. T	8. F	12. T	

page 74

1. T	5. T	9. T	13. F
2. T	6. F	10. F	14. F
3. T	7. T	11. F	15. T
4. F	8. T	12. T	

page 75

1. S	4. S	7. D	10. S
2. D	5. S	8. S	
3. D	6. S	9. D	

page 76

1. S	4. D	7. S	10. S
2. D	5. D	8. D	
3. S	6. S	9. D	

page 77

1. S	4. D	7. D	10. S
2. D	5. S	8. S	
3. S	6. D	9. D	

pages 78-82
Answers will vary. Guard against all items being answered "Yes."

page 83

page 84
mug #5

page 85
#2 gray cat

page 86
#2 recliner

page 87
#5 humanitarian trip

page 89
1. 2
2. 72
3. mailbox
4. fence
5. no
6. yes

7. round
8. 6
9. tire
10. picnic table

page 90
1. night
2. sofa, rocker, plant stand/table, TV stand
3. pillow
4. picture
5. kitchen
6. plant, picture, couch
7. no
8. rocker
9. blanket, afghan
10. cat

page 91
1. 6
2. clock, cupboards
3. 5:00
4. before
5. 6
6. spaghetti, salad
7. no
8. no
9. stove
10. pots

page 92
1. no
2. window, nightstand, alarm clock, poster
3. sneakers
4. clothing
5. poster
6. no
7. 7:00
8. glass
9. shut
10. toy car

page 93
1. alley
2. bike
3. squirrel
4. flowers
5. rectangle
6. trowel, hoe
7. flower
8. unplanted
9. 9
10. rain

page 94
1. Saturday
2. dusted
3. vacuum
4. throw rug
5. burning rubber
6. belt tore
7. kitchen drawer
8. Vernon
9. later that week
10. Answers will vary.

page 95
1. weekdays
2. bathroom time
3. got dressed
4. coffee, bagels, fruit
5. *school lunches* = more than one lunch; *children* means more than one child

6. cereal
7. books, lunches
8. Mom and Dad
9. drove to work
10. Answers will vary.

page 96
1. He was having company.
2. 450°
3. six
4. cinnamon, nutmeg
5. ready-made
6. dotted the apples with butter
7. ten minutes
8. 350°
9. 50 minutes
10. Andy's company

HOME MAINTENANCE ACTIVITIES

page 98
hinge, folding ruler, screwdriver, hammer, hard hat, scraper, creeper, caulking gun, drill

page 99
drill bit, putty knife, sledgehammer, wrench, plane, level, pliers, circular saw, screw

page 100
wrench, outlet, tape measure, extension light, pulley, scaffold, tin snips, C-clamp, molly/toggle bolt

page 101

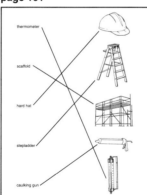

page 102

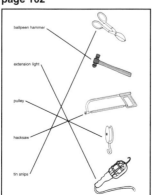

page 103

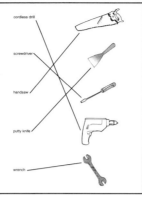

page 104
countersink
circuit breaker
claw hammer
drywall
hardware store
caulking gun
wing nut
rain gutter
sump pump
soldering iron
extension cord
pressure-treated wood
toggle bolt
thumbtack
electric drill

page 105
machine screw
putty knife
sandpaper
smoke detector
ballpeen hammer
tin snips
pilot hole
door jamb
screwdriver
lawn mower
stepladder
power tools
paintbrush
saw blade
hedge trimmer

page 106
monkey wrench
latex paint
snow blower
sledgehammer
needlenose pliers
paint roller
duct tape
fiberglass insulation
Venetian blinds
3-prong plug
Phillips head screwdriver
chain saw
plumber's snake
ceramic tile
staple gun

page 107
1. h   4. i   7. k   10. c
2. g   5. b   8. d   11. l
3. a   6. f   9. e   12. j

page 108
1. d   4. a   7. l   10. e
2. j   5. g   8. f   11. b
3. h   6. k   9. c   12. i

page 109
1. f   4. h   7. e   10. l
2. i   5. b   8. c   11. j
3. a   6. d   9. g   12. k

page 110
1. saw
2. brick, wood, stone
3. posts, wood, wire
4. hammer, saw, wood
5. screwdriver
6. cement
7. plumber
8. linoleum, hardwood, tile
9. paint, stain, varnish
10. caulking, grout
11. lamp, extension light
12. shovel, post hole digger
13. landscaper, gardener
14. plunger, chemical drain cleaner, plumber's snake
15. water, paint thinner

page 111
1. hammer
2. remote control
3. wires, screwdriver, wire stripper, needlenose pliers
4. fertilizer, water, weed killer
5. carpet, varnish, wax
6. clippers, weed whacker, edger
7. shovel, snow blower
8. roofer
9. clamp, vise
10. dehumidifier
11. mortar
12. thermostat
13. workshop, basement, garage
14. sandpaper
15. lighter, match, auto start

page 112
1. lawn mower
2. air conditioner, fan
3. architect, contractor
4. garage, parking lot
5. porch, sunroom
6. drill
7. wood
8. pipes, wrench
9. gutter
10. rake, leaf blower
11. spackle, plaster, putty
12. wood, brick, stone
13. salt
14. thermometer
15. ladder

page 113
1. roof
2. boards
3. door
4. ladder
5. saw
6. wall
7. plug
8. ruler

9. ceiling
10. brush
11. flashlight
12. screw
13. jar, paint can
14. louvered door, window blinds
15. sink
16. toolbox
17. wrench
18. drill
19. saw
20. mower
21. cord
22. roof
23. pipes
24. chimney
25. car
26. sidewalk
27. hammer, shower
28. nut and bolt
29. roof
30. hose

page 114
1. door
2. car
3. dryer
4. shower
5. stove
6. wall
7. wall
8. caulking gun
9. house, picture
10. stairs
11. vacuum cleaner
12. car
13. light
14. floor
15. window
16. outlet
17. stairs
18. sink
19. room
20. deck
21. phone
22. cement
23. workbench
24. heater
25. door, gate
26. window
27. radio, phone, TV
28. car radiator
29. bicycle
30. house, garage, workshop

page 115
1. yard
2. screw
3. black
4. rope
5. house
6. soldering iron
7. mansion
8. siren
9. stone
10. mile
11. penknife
12. chain saw
13. paint
14. masking tape
15. second

page 116
1. inch
2. beam
3. steel
4. spotlight
5. drywall
6. glass
7. dry ice
8. tree
9. sandpaper
10. beep
11. tar
12. tape rule
13. backhoe
14. plywood
15. saw

page 117
Lawn: mower, grass seed, fertilizer, water
Painting: brushes, paint, roller, drop cloth
Bookshelves: wood, nails, hammer, stain
Barbecuing: grill, meat, coals, spatula

page 118
Wall: spackle, putty knife, sandpaper, paint
Step: wood, hammer, nails, saw
Picture: picture, hammer, nail, picture hanger
Car: oil, wax, washer fluid, inspections

page 120
Carpentry Words
1. saw
2. wood
3. stain
4. joint
5. varnish
6. clamp
7. dowel
8. bond
9. bevel
10. wedge

Tool Words
1. chisel
2. trowel
3. drill
4. hammer
5. level
6. plane
7. pliers
8. screwdriver
9. tin snips
10. wrench

page 121
Electricity Words
1. watt
2. fuse
3. shock
4. cord
5. power
6. spark
7. plug
8. wire
9. amps
10. switch

Home Repair Words
1. paint
2. caulk
3. grout
4. sand
5. glue
6. oil
7. polish
8. stain
9. scrape
10. tighten

page 122
Wallpapering Words
1. water
2. wall
3. paper
4. strips
5. ladder
6. rolls
7. seam
8. pattern
9. brush
10. knife

Home Appliances
1. stove
2. can opener
3. clock radio
4. microwave
5. coffeemaker
6. toaster
7. washer
8. refrigerator
9. dishwasher
10. dryer

page 123
1. A tape rule is used for measuring.
2. Asphalt is used in paving mixtures.
3. A wing nut has flared sides.
4. A sump pump drains away excess water.
5. Stain is used to color wood.
6. Be careful when handling broken glass.
7. Most toilets are made out of porcelain.
8. Do not reuse disposable vacuum bags.
9. Cupboard doors are held closed by latches.
10. A washer can help fix a leaky faucet.

page 124
1. Is the lightbulb out?
2. Try tightening the nut with a wrench.
3. Place a ladder on firm level ground.
4. Do not grind glass in your garbage disposal.
5. A dresser drawer slides on runners.
6. Sealer is used to close holes.
7. Plywood is made of layers of veneer.
8. Solder is used to join metal parts.
9. Toggle bolts can be used to hang pictures.
10. Smoke and hot air go up a chimney.

page 125
1. Many homes are covered in aluminum siding.
2. A workshop can be located in the basement.
3. Support planks on sawhorses when cutting.
4. Use a dustpan and brush for cleanup.
5. Sandpaper is used to smooth wood.
6. Spray squeaky hinges with a lubricating compound.
7. A smoke detector warns against fire.
8. Paint blisters can appear on a wall.
9. If the lights go out, check the circuit breaker.
10. Carpenters usually choose screws for repairs.

page 126
soot, flashlight, condition, rusty, with, brush, damper, ease, expert, never, closed

page 127
space, kitchen, solve, large, cook, steps, another, removing, size, expensive, everything

page 128
electric, plug, frayed, loose, circuit, tripped, outlet, lamp, fails, electrician, fix

page 129
rivets, hole, material, through, end, flatten, tool, spread, petals, hold, place

page 130
Set A: 4, 2, 5, 1, 3
unclogging a drain
Set B: 5, 1, 3, 4, 2
mowing the lawn
Set C: 3, 5, 2, 4, 1
hanging a picture
Set D: 3, 1, 2, 5, 4
painting a room

page 131
Set A: 2, 5, 4, 1, 6, 3
gluing a broken plate
Set B: 3, 1, 6, 4, 2, 5
replacing a plank on a wooden porch
Set C: 2, 5, 3, 6, 1, 4
planting a vegetable garden
Set D: 5, 1, 6, 3, 2, 4
washing/waxing a car

page 132
Set A: 2, 1, 3
  replacing a fluorescent
  lightbulb
Set B: 3, 2, 1
  lubricating the track of
  a sliding door
Set C: 1, 3, 2
  fixing a doorknob
Set D: 2, 3, 4, 1
  hanging a mirror

page 133
1st check what you have at home
2nd make a list
3rd go to hardware store
4th paint bedroom
5th clean up
6th wash down the walls
7th wallpaper the bathroom
8th caulk the bathtub
9th clean up the bathroom
Last: game and a nap

page 134
8:00 get up, shower, eat
  breakfast
9:00 post office
9:30 Farm and Family Center
10:00 gas station
10:30 bank
11:00 AutoStore
11:30 hardware store
12:00 home improvement center

page 136
Hand tools: hammer, saw,
  pliers, wrench, level, chisel,
  file, screwdriver
Plumber: pipes, wrench, pliers,
  snake, hammer, drain cleaner,
  elbow joints, faucet
Car: battery, exhaust pipe,
  steering wheel, windshield,
  tires, trunk, hood, engine

page 137
Cut: handsaw, chain saw,
  hacksaw, scissors, shears, tin
  snips, pipe cutter, box cutter,
  utility knife
Toolbox: hammer, nuts, electrical
  tape, scissors, bolts, pliers,
  screwdriver, level, pencil
Lawn care: mower, edger, hedge
  trimmer, shovel, hoe, trowel,
  rake, leaf blower, grass seed

page 138
Construction: contractor,
  plumber, electrician, mason,
  carpenter, painter, architect,
  roofer
Hardware store: tools, hardware,
  trash cans, batteries, cords,
  shovel, brooms, paint, brushes
Electrician: wires, pliers, wrench,
  wire cutters, ladder, switches,
  outlets, screws

page 139
Hammer: ballpeen, head, claw,
  nails, handle
Lawn: mower, fertilizer, rye grass,
  edging, crab grass
toolbox: lid, tools, latch, handle,
  carry
Attic: rafters, hot, beams, roof,
  storage
Car: fender, dipstick, radiator,
  muffler, battery
Carpentry: wood, nails, sanding,
  hammer, cupboards

page 140
Building materials: brick, wood,
  cement, stone, concrete
Electricity: watts, wires, current,
  cord, amps
Hardware: nails, hinges, screws,
  washers, bolts
Woods: oak, pine, cherry,
  mahogany, walnut
Tools: chisel, hammer, wrench,
  punch, pliers
Painting: roller, thinner, paint,
  brush, drop cloth

page 141
Electrical words: switch, circuit,
  volts, outlet, current, watts,
  wire
Metals: iron, gold, brass, steel,
  tin, copper, aluminum, silver
Things that cut: razor, tin snips,
  plane, jigsaw, hacksaw, box
  cutter, shears
Parts of a truck: exhaust, engine,
  windshield, suspension, bed,
  windows, roof
Measurements: inch, meter,
  yard, ton, foot, pound, mile,
  ounce

page 142
Painting words: roller, primer,
  drop cloth, brush, drips, latex,
  thinner
Plumbing: water, faucet, drains,
  pipes, toilet, sink, shower
Tools: saw, punch, plane, pliers,
  wrench, chisel, hammer, awl
Parts of a house: hallway,
  bedroom, stairs, walls,
  kitchen, basement, roof,
  bathroom
Carpentry words: nails, lathe,
  wood, plane, sander, boards,
  varnish

page 143
Laborers and workers: plumber,
  roofer, painter, mason,
  contractor, electrician,
  landscaper
Lawn care: fertilizer, watering,
  weed killer, edging, mowing,
  seeding, trimming
Things in a garage: shovel,
  broom, shelves, rake, car,
  flowerpots, hoe, bucket

Building material: cement, stone,
  brick, concrete, steel, iron,
  wood, tile
Cleaning items: shop vac,
  dustpan, rags, vacuum,
  broom, mop, towels

page 144
1. measuring tools
2. paint
3. professions
4. hardware
5. wood finishes
6. tools
7. stores
8. metals
9. paint supplies
10. garden tools
11. woods, trees
12. measurements
13. building materials
14. types of saws
15. things that cut

page 145
1. parts of a house
2. insects, pests
3. containers
4. hammers
5. screwdrivers
6. building materials
7. lawn/lawn care items
8. supports in a building
9. cleaning items/supplies
10. types of screws
11. electrical items
12. plumber's tools
13. lubricants
14. types of wrenches
15. safety clothing

page 146
1. ladders
2. stones
3. wall coverings, wallboards
4. things hung on the wall
5. masonry tools
6. heat sources
7. clear wood finishes
8. used to hold things
9. floor coverings
10. things that are measured
11. corrosion, deterioration
  in a house
12. things that can be tied
13. types of shrubs/hedges
14. nails
15. glues

page 148
1. sandpaper
2. screwdriver
3. fence
4. plug
5. hinge
6. scissors
7. paintbrush
8. paint
9. hammer
10. roof
11. chimney
12. sink
13. varnish
14. wrench
15. car

page 149
1. extension cord
2. fan
3. bulb
4. wheelbarrow
5. nail
6. saw
7. ladder
8. garden
9. boots
10. thermostat
11. broom
12. lawn mower
13. rust
14. knob
15. drill

page 150
1. thermometer
2. hard hat
3. clamp
4. spackle
5. plane
6. ax
7. tar
8. canvas
9. duct tape
10. plunger
11. wallpaper
12. scale
13. bucket
14. saw, knife
15. ruler, yardstick

page 151
1. wrench
2. cook
3. glass
4. rafters
5. nail
6. damper
7. pipes
8. paper
9. brick
10. sandpaper
11. card
12. can
13. beam
14. oil
15. pole

page 152
1. roll
2. linoleum
3. rose
4. shed
5. seesaw
6. plank
7. wheel
8. train
9. sieve
10. pool
11. steel
12. paper
13. age
14. firm
15. tape worm

page 153
sockets
screwdriver
folding ruler
mallet

page 154
circular saw
scissors
lock
pencil

page 155
1. wall
2. strikes
3. bristles
4. glass
5. stick
6. part
7. wires
8. round
9. seal
10. rattle
11. claw
12. pliers
13. kitchen
14. whitening
15. summer

page 156
1. fan, mower
2. eyes
3. wood
4. smoothing
5. wrench
6. light, bright
7. metal
8. metal
9. trim
10. cools
11. roof
12. stairway
13. socket
14. solid walls
15. wood

page 157
1. handle/washer
2. rubber cement/grout
3. hinge/molly or toggle
4. varnish/veneer
5. rain spout/chimney
6. silicone/canvas
7. plaster/metal
8. plane/ballpeen, type of hammer/used to shave or smooth wood
9. hose/jack
10. electrician/plumber, plumbing/electrical

page 158
1. alcohol/water
2. ten/four
3. hedge trimmer/ax, chain saw, cut down a tree/trim bushes
4. concrete/wood
5. nail/bolt
6. ladder/wrench, hammer
7. clock/drain
8. calf/waist
9. wrench/hammer, drive in nails/tighten bolts
10. 5,000/2,000

page 159
1. slippers/boots
2. safe/dangerous, uneven loose gravel/firm ground
3. Styrofoam/wood
4. teeth/fingers
5. joist/joint
6. circular saw/hedge trimmer, trim bushes/cut boards
7. rubber/ceramic
8. heat/cool
9. sawdust/bricks
10. plumber's snake/screwdriver, open paint cans/clear a clogged drain

page 160
1. F 5. T 9. T 13. T
2. T 6. F 10. T 14. T
3. T 7. F 11. F 15. T
4. F 8. T 12. F

page 161
1. F 5. T 9. T 13. F
2. T 6. T 10. F 14. T
3. F 7. F 11. T 15. T
4. T 8. F 12. F

page 162
1. T 5. T 9. F 13. T
2. T 6. F 10. T 14. F
3. F 7. F 11. T 15. F
4. T 8. T 12. T

page 163
1. F 5. T 9. F 13. F
2. T 6. T 10. T 14. T
3. T 7. F 11. T 15. F
4. F 8. T 12. F

page 164
1. T 5. F 9. T 13. F
2. F 6. T 10. F 14. T
3. F 7. T 11. F 15. T
4. T 8. F 12. T

page 165
1. S 4. D 7. D 10. S
2. S 5. D 8. S
3. D 6. S 9. D

page 166
1. S 4. S 7. D 10. D
2. D 5. D 8. S
3. D 6. S 9. S

page 167
1. S 4. S 7. D 10. S
2. D 5. S 8. S
3. D 6. D 9. D

page 168
1. No   6. Yes 11. Yes
2. Yes 7. Yes 12. Yes
3. Yes 8. No   13. No
4. No   9. Yes 14. Yes
5. No   10. No 15. Yes

page 169
1. No   6. No   11. Yes
2. Yes 7. Yes 12. Yes
3. No   8. Yes 13. No
4. No   9. No   14. No
5. Yes 10. No 15. Yes

page 170
1. Yes 6. No   11. No
2. Yes 7. Yes 12. Yes
3. No   8. No   13. No
4. No   9. Yes 14. Yes
5. Yes 10. No 15. No

page 171
1. No   6. Yes 11. Yes
2. No   7. No   12. No
3. Yes 8. Yes 13. No
4. Yes 9. No   14. Yes
5. Yes 10. No 15. No

page 172
1. Yes 6. Yes 11. No
2. No   7. Yes 12. No
3. Yes 8. No   13. Yes
4. Yes 9. No   14. No
5. No   10. Yes 15. Yes

page 173
curved claw

page 174
round self-rimming sink

page 175
B. bent-handle standard duty shears

page 176
Rex–basement
Chris–supervisor
Skip–attic
Bob–porch

page 177
Pete–plumber
Paul–painter
Pat–roofer
Preston–mason

plumbing–Tony, Alice
landscaping–Candie, Jack

page 179
1. painting
2. bedroom
3. paint, roller, paint tray, stepladder, drop cloths
4. paint can, roller, paint tray
5. roller
6. light blue
7. open
8. yes, mostly
9. bed, chair
10. no

page 180
1. bathroom
2. tiles
3. one
4. diamonds
5. yes
6. yes
7. yes
8. towel, shower curtain
9. plain
10. shampoo, soap dish, showerhead, shower handle, spigot

page 181
1. wall
2. two
3. nail
4. closed
5. on the floor
6. putty knife
7. lion/jungle
8. leaning against the wall
9. Tony's
10. throw rug

page 182
1. flowerpots
2. three
3. one
4. two
5. bush
6. on the sawhorses
7. gloves
8. no
9. handsaw
10. on the sidewalk

page 183
1. one
2. roof
3. on the ground
4. hammer, nails
5. two
6. window box
7. left window
8. boy
9. open
10. leaning on the house

page 184
1. underside, stringer supports
2. hardware or home improvement store
3. nail the new board in place
4. nail set
5. plastic wood, wood filler
6. paint or stain
7. from a store clerk, reference book, the Internet
8. Answers will vary.

page 185
1. collect moisture, sweat
2. condensation
3. fiberglass insulation
4. hardware or building supply store
5. waterproof
6. once
7. add a waterproof wrapping
8. Answers will vary.

page 186
1. three
2. two
3. silicone lubricant
4. where risers meet the tread
5. between the tread and stringer
6. screws
7. finishing nails
8. along the tread into the stringer
9. Answers will vary.